God is the Light of the heavens and earth.
The parable of His Light is as if there were a Niche,
and within it a Lamp —
the Lamp is in Glass, the Glass as it were a brilliant Star,
lit by a blessed Tree, an Olive-tree, neither of the East nor the West —
whose Oil almost glows, even though fire has not touched it.
Light upon Light!
God guides to His Light whomever He wishes,
God makes parables for people,
And God is Aware of everything.

(Âyat al-Nûr, "The Light Verse," *Qur'ân* 24:35)

ISLAM

A Short Guide to the Faith

edited by

Roger Allen *&* Shawkat M. Toorawa

WILLIAM B. EERDMANS PUBLISHING COMPANY
GRAND RAPIDS, MICHIGAN / CAMBRIDGE, U.K.

Published 2011 by
Wm. B. Eerdmans Publishing Co.
2140 Oak Industrial Drive N.E., Grand Rapids, Michigan 49505 /
P.O. Box 163, Cambridge CB3 9PU U.K.

Printed in the United States of America

17 16 15 14 13 12 11   7 6 5 4 3 2 1

Library of Congress Cataloging-in-Publication Data

Islam: a short guide to the faith / edited by Roger Allen & Shawkat M. Toorawa.
    p.   cm.
Includes bibliographical references and index.
ISBN 978-0-8028-6600-4 (pbk.: alk. paper)
1. Islam — Essence, genius, nature. 2. Islam — Doctrines.
3. Islam — 21st century.   I. Allen, Roger M.A.   II. Toorawa, Shawkat M.

  BP165.I74 2011
  297 — dc22

              2010044115

www.eerdmans.com

Contents

III. DOCTRINE

IV. INSTITUTIONS

V. INTERACTIONS

Foreword

Bruce B. Lawrence

Religion, according to most authorities, escapes definition, yet each religion has defining elements. They are: discourse, practices, community, and institution. No religion can be understood apart from a discourse that merges mundane facts, and human needs, with transcendent aims and celestial hopes. The discourse cannot succeed without practices that aim to engage the believer, and reinforce good behavior, with results in this world that are matched by rewards in the next. Yet no believer operates in isolation, and it is the ethos of a collective cohort, a group or community, that provides options, and also reinforces discipline, for each individual bounded within its arc of influence and marked by its public identity. Institutions, in turn, attend to all the defining elements of religion: they regulate discourse, they enforce practices, and they project community, not without human error or self-correction but always with a commitment to continuity and self-perpetuation beyond the lifetime of individuals or movements or nations.*

*   *   *

In this perceptive yet compressed set of essays, the general reader is introduced to all four constitutive elements of religion as they have found ex-

*I have adopted the categories of Bruce Lincoln (*Holy Terrors: Thinking about Religion after September 11* [Chicago: University of Chicago Press, 2003], pp. 5-7), but modified them to reflect my own sense of how these four defining elements of religion relate to one another, and to society as a whole.

pression, and persisted for almost 1,400 years, under the banner of Islam. The frame essay makes clear that Islam is normal. It does not claim to shape the entire lives of those defined, by themselves and by others, as Muslim. What distinguishes Muslims from other people of faith is beliefs linked to specific origins: the seventh-century Prophet who was an Arab merchant living near the Red Sea; the protracted and contested set of revelations given to that Prophet, then collected and assembled as a book, the Noble Book, the Holy Qur'an; and then the science of trying to understand both the book and the Prophet through instruments of memory (Hadith) that provide a composite profile of good behavior and social integrity for all Muslims (Sunna).

The section on origins provides the basis for the subsequent development of Islam as both a discourse and a set of practices. The two are closely intertwined through the emergence of three trajectories of knowledge: the Shari'a, which acts as a template for encoding and enforcing the tenets of Islam; philosophy, which interjects reason, or *'aql,* as the necessary complement and occasional corrective to tradition, or *naql;* and Sufism, which stresses that external rules, acts, words cannot substitute for inner purity, intention, and passion. There can be no Islam without Shari'a, but Shari'a is challenged by philosophy and amplified by Sufism in a way that enriches each branch of discourse and makes possible multiple avenues of Muslim practice. It is Sunnis and Shi'ites who compete to represent the ethos of Islam in its original, pristine formulation. While sharing the same Prophet and the same Noble Book, they differ on the way the Prophet is remembered through Hadith, and also on the way his family and descendants *(ahl al-bayt)* are connected to the subsequent emergence of Islamic empire.

The key institutions of Islamic empire, at once evoking discourse, confirming practices, and projecting a collective ethos, are mosque and government. They are inseparable, and have been so from the earliest times. When the newly converted Arabs conquered the former territories of the Byzantine Empire, Muslim leaders saw numerous monuments to Christian architectural achievement that were worthy of emulation. Above all, in greater Syria there were still some forested areas with timber as yet unfelled and plentiful supplies of fine building stone, together with a human tradition of building skills and fine craftsmanship. The presence of these factors favored the erection of imposing Islamic public buildings and private palaces throughout the region. Vast construction projects begun by the Umayyads marked their dynasty in Damascus, just as subsequent projects marked the Abbasids in Baghdad, the defecting Umayyads in Andalusia (Islamic Spain), and the later major empires of Ottoman, Safavid, and Mughal lineage. Islamic public piety became inseparable from monumental mosques and also from buildings marking the death of illustrious figures, whether the Imam ʿAlî shrine in Najaf or the Taj Mahal, built for the Mughal queen Nur Jahan, in Agra.

Equally important for understanding the scope and durability of Islam are relations between Muslims and non-Muslims. Again, one must begin with discourse: the verses of the Qur'an both extol and critique those people of faith who preceded the Prophet and the emergence of a new Abrahamic community marked as Muslim. Sayings of the Prophet confirmed, but also often contrasted with, the tone of the Qur'anic dispensation, with the most decisive element being the role of institutions, and especially Muslim political leaders, in their attitude toward non-Muslims. The question from the earliest days was: How were Muslim rulers, as custodians of Islam and enforcers of public piety, to deal with conquered populations that included non-Muslim religious minorities? Like their Byzantine and late Sassanian predecessors, the Umayyad caliphs nominally ruled the various religious communities while allowing the communities' own appointed or elected officials to administer most internal affairs. Both the Qur'an and Sunna justified this modus vivendi: as peoples with revealed books *(ahl al-kitâb)*, Jews and Christians deserved protection *(dhimma)* in return for a payment. The Arabs themselves formed a single religious community whose right to rule over the non-Arab protected communities, the Umayyad caliphs and later their Abbasid successors sought to maintain. The same delicate protocol did not always pertain. There were ugly moments of religiously inscribed warfare — the Crusades in the Levant and the counter-Crusades or Reconquista in Andalusia — that marred Muslim-Christian-Jewish relations, but the lasting merit of the original compact, as expressed in the Qur'an and most of Sunna, and also exemplified in the policy of the earliest caliphs, continues to be evident today. It is amply detailed in the final three chapters of this splendid introduction to Islam.

One entire chapter is also devoted to women. In the many ways that Islam has been portrayed, the Muslim view of women, as also the rights and roles of Muslim women, has perhaps been the most misunderstood. Without Khadîja, the Prophet's first wife, there would have been no Noble Book and hence no Islam. Working for Khadîja gave the Prophet opportunity to travel and to reflect. When revelation came, Khadîja was the first to accept this new role for her trustworthy but now benighted spouse. The

Noble Book accords women rights that were not common, or accepted, in early-seventh-century Arabia. Yet after Khadîja died, the Prophet married again, not once but several times, and the memories of his life recorded in Hadith do not grant women the same high favor as the Noble Book. Yet the Shariʿa has balanced the two scriptural streams that flow together in sustaining the reflection and buttressing the authority of its agents, the ʿulamâ', or fuqahâ', the scholars and jurists, whose domain is the law. Women not only have inheritance and property rights, they can also make demands of their fiancés prior to marriage in a prenuptial contract that is then enforceable, even in times of marital stress.

It is the dress code of women, more than polygamy or women's rights, that has obsessed recent portrayals of Islam and gender. A non-Arab, likely Byzantine practice, veiling, along with building royal monuments, was embraced by conquering Muslim elites; both became part and parcel of an urban, cosmopolitan Muslim way of life. Transformations from the eighteenth century on, marked as European invasion, colonial rule, and postcolonial governance, have highlighted the veil as a native form of dress, one that evokes nostalgia for the integrity of an earlier era. This historical memory, combined with competing interpretations of Qur'anic verses and memories of Prophetic guidance (hadiths), has fueled the debate about the veil. It will continue, but it should not dominate or distort the other legacies of Islam: an inclusive worldview, an urban-based exploration of knowledge, an urbane sense of ethics and justice, and above all, a creativity and generosity of spirit, marked most strikingly by Sufism but also by the pervasive resilience of ordinary Muslims in the myriad contexts that define their piebald global community.

*   *   *

The reader will find in the following chapters well-crafted and highly accessible essays that depict the broad elements, together with the specific accents, that make Islam like other religions, but also distinctive in its historical and contemporary expression. While complexities abound, the chapters individually and collectively provide a path to understanding and dealing with them. This book is a reliable guide, an exceptional window, into a faith more important today than at any moment in the recent past.

Editors' Preface

Roger Allen & Shawkat M. Toorawa

In 2008, Norman Hjelm approached Roger Allen with the suggestion that he edit a text on Islam, using as a basis for the book several articles already published by Eerdmans, including Roger Allen's own "Qur'an." Roger Allen then approached Shawkat Toorawa to see whether he was interested in coediting such a volume. We both agreed to do so, motivated in large part by the possibility of producing an introductory text on Islam that was an edited volume, that is to say, one in which aspects of Islam are addressed by different experts, rather than the far more common single-authored text.

Of the existing articles proposed by Eerdmans, we elected to retain "Shi'ites, Shi'ism," "Shari'a," "Sufism," "Islam and Christianity," and "Islam in America"; we showed these articles to colleagues who are experts on the respective topics and incorporated suggestions they proposed. "Hadith and Sunna" and "Sunnis, Sunnism" we reworked with the author's blessing; we commissioned "Muhammad," "Mosque," "Islamic Philosophy," "Islamic Government," "Women and Islam," and "Islam and Judaism"; and Shawkat Toorawa wrote "Islam." In all cases we edited for style, format, and, where necessary, content; and we updated and augmented the accompanying bibliographies.

The volume has been shaped in part by the articles suggested by the publisher, but in the main by what we deemed to be the most important aspects of Islam for a contemporary North American reader. There are undoubtedly other areas we could have profitably covered, in particular in the arts and literature, areas close to our hearts and expertise. We decided, for better or worse, to focus on matters relating to Islam as a system of religious beliefs, rather than on Islam as a culture and civilization — that would have required a book that plumbed deeper and surveyed more widely. In view of this, we have tried to produce a wide-ranging bibliography of further reading and viewing.

Each essay is relatively short. Our aim is to provide the reader the opportunity to read an authoritative survey on a given apect of Islam in an unburdensome piece. Each is self-standing, but cross-reference is made where appropriate to other essays in the volume. There is also a glossary of significant non-English words, and some recurring names, mentioned in the text.

Acknowledgments

This book has benefited from the expertise of numerous individuals and would have been poorer but for their involvement. We should like to express our gratitude to:

The contributors, for allowing us to edit, and intervene in, their concise, readable, and informative chapters as we saw fit; Ross Brann, Jamal Elias, Sidney Griffith, Sherman Jackson, Joe Lowry, and Devin Stewart, for carefully looking over several of the articles at our request; Bruce Lawrence, for a splendid Foreword; Franklin Robinson, Director, Ellen Avril, Chief Curator, and Elizabeth Emrich, Rights Manager, Herbert F. Johnson Museum of Art, Cornell University, for permission to use four images of Museum artwork, including the Qur'an folio that graces the front cover; Saqib Hasan for two photographs taken during his travels; David and Susan Owen for permission to use a piece in their private collection, and Laura Johnson-Kelly for photographing that piece; David Toorawa for a photograph from his private collection; Holly Frisbee, Permissions Manager, Philadelphia Museum of Art, for permission to use the image that adorns the back cover, and Kaila Bussert and Fiona Patrick at Olin Library, Cornell University, for assistance in obtaining it; Boris Michov and Nij Tontisirin, Maps & Geospatial Information Collection, Olin Library, Cornell University, the former for genial assistance and the latter for generously invested hours of design on the color map showing up-to-date information on Muslim populations worldwide; Maryam Toorawa for yeoman's work on the index; Linda Bieze, Tom Raabe, Willem Mineur, Klaas Wolsterstorff, and the staff at Eerdmans, for input and assistance with all aspects of production; Bill Eerdmans for conceiving of and for patronizing this small but important project; and Norman Hjelm for being the project's guardian angel.

Note to Readers

Pronunciation

The words "Islam," "Muslim," and "Allah" are routinely mispronounced. The *s* in "Islam" and "Muslim" (and all Arabic words rendered into English) is not pronounced as a *z*, as in the word "reason," but as an *s*, as in the word "base." Also, the *a* in "Islam" is long. Thus, the two syllables of "Islam" are pronounced "Iss" (to rhyme with English "kiss") and "laam" (to rhyme with English "jam"), giving what might be more accurately rendered as "Iss-laam."

In the word "Muslim," the first syllable rhymes with English "Puss," and the second syllable is "lim," giving "Muss-lim."

In the word "Allah," the first syllable rhymes with the English word "gull" and the second is pronounced like the musical note "La" (with a long *a*), giving what might be more accurately rendered as "Ull-laa."

Rendering of Arabic words

We use a very simplified system, designed *solely* to assist with pronunciation. In most words we have indicated the long vowels with a circumflex, thus *muhâjirûn* for a word to be pronounced "muhaajiroon," and *kitâb* for a word to be pronounced "kitaab".

If a word has entered the English language, we retain its accepted spelling, for example, Islam, Qur'an, Shi'ite. As the last two examples show, we also retain the apostrophe and inverted apostrophe to represent 'ayn and *hamza,* two sounds that do not have equivalents in the English alphabet.

Names

Names of individuals, such as Ibn Khaldûn, are often mistakenly interpreted as first name Ibn, last name Khaldûn. To avoid confusion we have hyphenated such names, thus Ibn-Sîna, rather than Ibn Sîna. For the sake of consistency, we also hyphenate other types of Arabic names, for example, 'Umar-ibn-al-Khattâb.

Dates

We have elected to use common era dates throughout the main text.

Qur'an references

References to the Qur'an appear as follows: "Q 1:3," where the "Q" indicates that the reference is to the Qur'an, the "1" is the chapter number, and "3" the verse number.

Translations from the Qur'an cited in the essays are by the respective authors, unless otherwise indicated.

PART I

INTRODUCTION

Chapter One

ISLAM

Shawkat M. Toorawa

Islam — in Arabic, literally, "submission" or "surrender" (to the will of God) — is a monotheistic religion professed by over 1.5 billion people worldwide. Adherents of Islam are called Muslims. South Asia (Bangladesh, India, and Pakistan) is home to some 480 million Muslims, and a similar number are to be found in North Africa, the Middle East, Iran, Turkey, and central Asia. Sub-Saharan Africa has some 240 million Muslims (with large populations in Nigeria and Ethiopia), and Southeast Asia has 220 million Muslims (principally in Indonesia, and also Malaysia). The remaining 600 million or so are scattered across the globe, including 16 million in Russia and 20 million in China. Though not significant in number, the Muslims of western Europe (10 million) and North America (3.5 million) wield considerable symbolic and intellectual power in contemporary discourses in and about Islam. The desire of Muslim women to wear the head covering (the *hijâb*) in France and Germany, for instance, has seriously tested those countries' purportedly unswerving commitment to freedom of expression and of religion. And scholars of Islam, both Muslim and non-Muslim, in the United States and England in particular, have contributed to a rethinking (some would say reformation) in their discussions about Islamic law and practice. Muslims in North America, many of whom are professionals, exert considerable influence on Muslims in other parts of the world through their wealth and resources (see "Islam in America," chapter 15). But it remains true that many of the areas where Islam has spread have inherited legacies of colonialism (e.g., most of the Middle East), state oppression (e.g., China, with anywhere from 20 million to 150 million Muslims), and economic hardship (e.g., in Africa); it is also true that the majority of Muslims are poor and have limited access to food, water, resources, health care, education, and self-determination. These severe constraints have inevitably shaped the desires and actions of many predominantly Muslim countries and some of their inhabitants.

Muslim Population by Region, 2009

	Estimated 2009 Muslim Population	Percentage of Population That Is Muslim	Percentage of World Muslim Population
Asia-Pacific	972,537,000	24.1	61.9
Middle East–North Africa	315,322,000	91.2	20.1
Sub-Saharan Africa	240,632,000	30.1	15.3
Europe	38,112,000	5.2	2.4
Americas	4,596,000	0.5	0.3
World Total	1,571,198,000	22.9	100.0

Source: "Mapping the Global Muslim Population: A Report on the Size and Distribution of the World's Muslim Population," October 2009; available online at www.pewforum.org/publications.

* * *

Beginnings

As in other religions, Muslims run the gamut, from extremely devout to lapsed, from extremist to ultraliberal, from converted to merely cultural, and of course everything in between. Virtually all self-identifying Muslims are bound together, however, by an acknowledgment of the existence of one God (a notion called *tawhîd* in Arabic) and by belief in the divine origin of the Qur'an as God's speech (see "Qur'an," chapter 2) and in the ministry of the Prophet Muhammad (see "Muhammad," chapter 3). Muhammad, son of 'Abdallah, was born in the pilgrimage and trading town of Mecca in about 570 into the influential Quraysh tribe, who were custodians of the Ka'ba, an ancient cube-shaped shrine. Muhammad's father died before he was born and his mother died when he was six years old; thereafter, the child was raised by his grandfather, and later his uncle, Abû-Tâlib.

A trader known for his honesty and integrity, Muhammad accepted the proposal of marriage from his wealthy widowed employer, Khadîja, when he was twenty-five years old and she perhaps as old as forty. Their close, loving relationship during their twenty-five-year marriage and Muhammad's affection for his four daughters — no sons survived infancy — are described by many, including Western feminists, as the basis for Muhammad's egalitarian stances on gender. It is certainly the case that Islam enfranchised women by granting them rights and autonomy hitherto denied to them in any political or religious system (see "Women and Islam," chapter 12). It is also true that Muhammad's numerous marriages, after Khadîja's death, form the basis for many detractors' criticisms of Islam's patrilineal regulations and acceptance of polygamy (if under stringent conditions). It should be pointed out, however, that the patriarchal practices in many societies that embraced Islam are blamed on Islam itself: Muhammad's decision to marry an older, twice-widowed woman, for example, is nowhere emulated today, because of cultural and social values unconnected to Islam, in spite of the religious imperative to emulate Muhammad in all ways possible (see below).

Although the form of the initial revelations Muhammad received from God through the archangel Gabriel — a strongly rhythmic, rhyming prose — resembled the pronouncements of local Arabian oracles, this message was not mundane, but centered rather on belief in the One God (in Arabic, *Allâh*), on charitable acts, on right action, and on preparation for the Day of Judgment. One early revelation states:

> *In the Name of God, Full of Compassion, Ever Compassionate*
> [1]By Time, endless, [2]Humanity is assuredly in a state of loss, [3]Except for those who believe, perform righteous acts, mutually enjoin Truth and mutually enjoin Steadfastness.

These revelations — the *Qur'ân,* literally "Recitation" — made it clear that God wanted to impart through Muhammad to the Arabs and to the world the same revelation God had imparted through Noah (Nûh) to his people, through Abraham (Ibrâhîm) to the inhabitants of Ur, and through Moses (Mûsâ) and Jesus ('Îsâ) to the Jews. The Qur'an refers to the recipients of these earlier revelations as "people of the scripture" or "people of the book" (*ahl al-kitâb*).

Muhammad initially preached his message — which he received piecemeal from God through Gabriel over the next twenty-three years —

to his intimates, and soon after to those who would become his closest confidants, including ʿAlî (his first cousin and future son-in-law) and Abû-Bakr (his future father-in-law). Like disciples, the men and women around Muhammad (called *Sâhâba,* Companions) scrupulously memorized the revelations he repeated to them (i.e., the Qur'an) and also prophetic traditions (hadiths) containing his words of advice, instruction, and admonishment. By following the prescriptions of the Qur'an and by emulating the actions and deeds of Muhammad expressed in the hadiths (which collectively came to be called the Sunna), Muslims honor the Qur'anic injunction to "obey God and His Prophet" (see "Hadith and Sunna," chapter 4). But that obedience came at a price, especially for the poor and marginalized among his followers in Mecca, who were ostracized, banished, and persecuted by the ruling non-Muslim elite. As in Christianity, Islam first appealed to the indigent and disenfranchised, and it has continued to do so throughout its history: a large number of American converts, for instance, are low on the socioeconomic ladder, and members of ethnic minorities, including prisoners — it was in prison that the Black Muslim leader Malcolm X discovered Islam.

Growth

In 615, Muhammad temporarily sent a small band of his persecuted followers to Abyssinia, where he knew they would receive fair treatment as the kingdom was ruled by the Negus, a benevolent ruler, and, as a Christian, a believer (see "Islam and Christianity," chapter 14). The Qur'an, and consequently Islam, distinguishes more between believers in God and unbelievers than it does between Muslims and non-Muslims; it also makes an important distinction between the righteous and just (e.g., the Negus) on the one hand, and the tyrant and oppressor (e.g., Pharaoh) on the other. In 622, Muhammad accepted an invitation to move to the northern oasis town of Yathrib and become its chief. The Meccan Muslims traveled there in small bands and came to be known as the "Emigrants" *(Muhâjirûn);* those welcoming them came to be known as the "helpers" *(Ansâr),* and the city came to be known as Madînat al-Nabî (City of the Prophet), or Medina for short. In Medina, Muhammad set about establishing a community proper. The Qur'anic revelations from 622 until Muhammad's death in 632 reflect his new role as leader of a body politic, the *umma* (community). Since Medina's population was religiously diverse, Muhammad drew up a charter to protect all parties. The Constitution of Medina guaranteed, among other things, religious freedom, the security of women, and stability between warring tribes. But internal tensions in Medina led the Jewish tribes to collaborate with the Meccans, whose conflict with Muhammad escalated from skirmishes to full-scale war. In 628, Muhammad quashed the Jewish tribes and their confederates, and signed a treaty with the Meccans (see "Islam and Judaism," chapter 13). In 630, Muhammad entered Mecca without bloodshed and proceeded immediately to the Ka'ba, whereupon he destroyed all the idols within and around it (in an echo of Abraham's similar act before leaving Ur).

Medina remained the capital of the nascent Islamic state, but the Prophet did return to his hometown to perform the Hajj pilgrimage in 631. Before or after pilgrimage, Muslims pay their respects at Muhammad's tomb in Medina by wishing upon him God's salutations and blessings; indeed, many Muslims do this every time they hear or utter his name. Although God is the sole focus of prayer, prostration, petition, and worship, Muhammad nevertheless constitutes a major locus of reverence. This is why perceived or real attacks on him, such as the cartoons commissioned by a Danish newspaper in 2005 (or Salman Rushdie's 1989 novel *The Satanic Verses*, which parodies Muhammad), provoke such visceral reactions among so many Muslims. At issue and at stake is not the permissibility of depicting Muhammad — a frieze of Muhammad continues, for example, to grace the Supreme Court building in Washington, D.C., and numerous illustrations of Muhammad accompany manuscripts, both religious and secular — but rather the perceived insult to an emissary of God.

In one hadith, Muhammad is described as responding to a request that he define "Submission" (i.e., Islam) as follows: "Submission is that you bear witness that there is no god but God and that Muhammad is His messenger *(shahâda)*, that you perform the (prescribed) ritual-prayers *(salât)*, that you fast the month of Ramadan *(sawm)*, that you pay the (prescribed) alms-tax on wealth *(zakât)*, and that you perform the pilgrimage to the Ka'ba if you are able *(hajj)*." These obligations have come to be known as the five pillars of Islam, though some denominations enumerate other obligations: loving the Prophet and his family *(ahl al-bayt)*, namely, his daughter Fâtima, her husband 'Alî, and their children Hasan and Husayn *(tawallî)*, and having antipathy for the enemies of the Prophet and his family *(tabarru')*. Some also include struggling in the cause of the religion *(jihâd)*. *Jihâd* has been widely used and abused, both as a term and as a course of action, by Muslims and non-Muslims alike. Like the term "na-

tional security," it can be used by hawkish, militaristic, embattled interpreters to perpetrate violence, prosecute wars, and divest citizens of "God-
given" rights; it can also be used by peace-loving, nonviolent, and sympathetic interpreters to defend borders, defuse conflicts, reassure citizens,
and enhance personal piety and spirituality.

The testimony that there is no deity except for (the one, true) God and
that Muhammad is his (final) messenger constitutes Islam's fundamental
doctrinal belief, a formulation known as the *shahâda*. The *shahâda* must
be uttered at least once in a Muslim's lifetime: those born Muslim do so
from early childhood; converts utter it to mark their acceptance of Islam.
This phrase, as well as phrases from the Qur'an, can be found adorning
people's homes and also major Muslim monuments, such as the Dome of
the Rock (built 691) in Jerusalem, Islam's oldest standing religious structure, and the Alhambra (built between 1338 and 1390) in Granada, though
this Spanish palace's inscriptions include secular aphorisms and poetry.

There are more elaborate creeds, such as the important "Detailed Articles of Belief," which states: "I believe in God, in His angels, in His scriptures, in His messengers, in the Last Day, in destiny, both good and bad,
and in resurrection after death." This creed reveals that Islam sees itself as
part of a continuous process of revelation on God's part of His will to humanity, through angels and prophets and scriptures. Thus, for Islam, Moses received the *Tawrât* (Torah, the Hebrew Bible), David (Dâwûd) the
Zabûr (Psalms), and Jesus the *Injîl* (the Evangel, or Gospel) from God.
They were prophets, as were Adam (with Eve, half of the first human couple), Noah, Abraham, Solomon (Sulaymân), and John the Baptist (Yahyâ),
to name only a handful of the 126,000 messengers Islamic tradition says
God sent to humankind. Other prominent characters include Satan —
not a fallen angel but a disobedient jinn (origin of the English "genie"),
another kind of creation that inhabits the earth and to whom the Qur'an
is also addressed; Mary (Maryam), the mother of Jesus; the Seven
Sleepers of Ephesus; and some nonbiblical individuals, such as Khidr, the
long-living tutor to the prophets, and Dhul-Qarnayn, an Alexander figure. It is not surprising, therefore, that the Qur'an accepts, co-opts, and,
in its own view, corrects the narratives to be found in earlier monotheistic
scriptures. From the very beginning, then, Muhammad preached Islam as
part of a larger grace from God to humankind. This helps to explain why
Muhammad was regarded as a renegade by some Christians in the Middle
Ages, or as the founder of a Jewish, Christian, or Judeo-Christian heresy
in some modern Western scholarship. It is clear that the message Muham-

mad preached had a profound effect on his listeners, both in form and content.

Muslims believe that Muhammad was, while still alive, transported into the presence of God; during this Night Journey and Ascension, God prescribed the five daily ritual-prayers *(salât, namâz)*, known by the times they are to be performed: predawn *(fajr)*, early afternoon *(zuhr)*, midafternoon *('asr)*, sunset *(maghrib)*, and nighttime *('ishâ')*. All observant Muslims perform these ritual-prayers, either alone or, if possible, in congregation (which is preferable). The Friday congregational prayer *(Jum'a)* — which always includes a sermon, one often used for propaganda, not just exhortation — is also an obligation. It must be performed in a designated place of congregation. Typically that place is a congregational mosque *(jâmi')*, but a campus hall or any clean open space may also be used — Muhammad emphasized that a distinguishing feature of Islam is the possibility of performing one's ritual-prayers anywhere, that is, without needing a sacred or sanctified place, though simple ritual washing *(wudû'*, ablutions, or *tayammum,* if earth is used instead of water) is a prerequisite to ritual practices (see "Mosque," chapter 10). Because the Qur'an asks believers to abandon work and hasten to the Friday services, Jum'a is therefore not unlike the Jewish Sabbath service or the Sunday Mass, and consequently countries with large Muslim populations declare Friday a holiday and make Friday-Saturday the weekend.

The prescribed alms, or *zakât,* are repeatedly enjoined in the Qur'an, as is the need for performing regular charity in general. What distinguishes *zakât* is that it is not voluntary, but a required 2½ percent tax specifically on accumulated wealth and goods (not income), which must be paid out by those who have such wealth to those who do not. In some countries, ministries or departments collect *zakât* from Muslim citizens and distribute it to the needy, and in others, benevolent organizations do so. *Zakât*'s literal meaning is "purification," which suggests that the redistribution of wealth it entails, besides being an important communal and fiscal act, cleanses the believer.

"Fasting is prescribed for you just as it was prescribed to those who came before you," says the Qur'an, implying Jews on Yom Kippur or Christians in Lent. Besides voluntary fasting on almost any day of the year, the obligatory fast *(sawm, siyâm, roza)* lasts the whole of Ramadan, the ninth lunar month, and entails abstaining from all food, drink, and sex from before first light until sunset. Although it is one of the five pillars, the obligation is relaxed for anyone who is unable to fast, such as the very young, the very old, the infirm, those who fall sick doing so, and the like. Ultimately, like all the obligations (except the pilgrimage), it is up to the Muslim herself to regulate observance. According to the Prophet Muhammad, virtue *(ihsân)* "is that you worship God as if you see Him, for even though you do not, He sees you," underscoring the importance placed in Islam on personal responsibility and on the personal and unmediated relationship between the believer and God. All Muslims may cultivate this relationship through pious devotion and righteous acts, but it is especially the focus of many *sûfî* practices (see "Sufism," chapter 7). For Sufis (loosely, mystics), the ultimate aim is proximity (even "union") with the divine. To achieve this, they engage in active remembrance of God, by intoning pious phrases, by reciting Qur'anic verses, and by engaging in other practices that induce a heightened state of awareness, such as chanting or, in one celebrated case, whirling. These practices have been frowned upon by more austere Muslims, who believe that one is saved from hellfire and guaranteed paradise by doing what is prescribed and permitted, and avoiding — and punishing those who engage in — what is forbidden, a category interpreted narrowly. Given that most areas of Muslim concentration outside the Arabian Peninsula adopted Islam because of the appeal of the more populist practices of the Sufis, this hard-line position is difficult to maintain (and may even be disingenuous).

The Hajj is the largest annual pilgrimage in the world: today it draws between two and three million Muslims during the Hajj season (in the twelfth month of the Islamic calendar), and an equal number during the rest of the year (a voluntary pious act called *'umra*). It takes place specifically in the sacred precincts around the Ka'ba (or *bayt Allâh*, "house of God") and around Mecca. But the Hajj is an obligation most Muslims will never fulfill given the resources and time required, though many set aside money their entire lives and then spend those savings to perform the Hajj. Pilgrims reenact rituals performed by Muhammad, all the while dressed in two pieces of unsewn cloth (men) or simple cotton garments (women). The garb is called *ihrâm*, which is the term also for the sacralized state it represents, during which sexual intercourse, the cutting or shaving of hair, and the use of scented products are forbidden. The rituals are based in large part on the movements and actions of Abraham, who is believed by Muslims to have rebuilt the Ka'ba, a "house" originally erected for the worship of the one true God but that had been turned by lapsed monotheists into an animist shrine. They include circumambulating the Ka'ba, hurrying between two hills in a reenactment of Hagar's search for water for her infant, the symbolic stoning of Satan, and conclude with the sacrifice of animals in emulation of Abraham's willingness to sacrifice his son.

Flowering

When Muhammad died in 632, Abû-Bakr, the father of Muhammad's wife 'Â'ishah and one of his closest Companions, announced to the Muslims of Medina, "Those of you who believe in God, know that He is Alive and Everlasting; those of you who believed in Muhammad, know that he is dead." That declaration set the tone for Abû-Bakr's two years as caliph (from the Arabic *khalîfa,* successor), an office he reluctantly accepted. Some Muslims believed Muhammad had designated 'Alî as his successor and objected to the naming of Abû-Bakr; others openly stated that their allegiance to Muhammad had died with Muhammad. Abû-Bakr courted the former and fought the latter, and by the time of his natural death in 634, the entire Arabian Peninsula was nominally Muslim. His successor, 'Umar, was chosen by a *shûrâ* (council), and over the next ten years oversaw, from the capital in Medina, the expansion of the *umma* into a veritable empire. In 636, the Persian Empire fell to the Muslims; in 637 so did Byzantine Syria, including Jerusalem, which remained under Muslim control from then until the British defeat of the Ottomans in 1917, except for an eighty-seven-year period during the Crusades.

Under Muslim rule (see "Islamic Government," chapter 11), all monotheists were protected: they enjoyed freedom of worship and congregation, and were allowed to engage in economic, artistic, and intellectual activity. Monasteries, for instance, thrived in Islamic lands; the most famous was St. Catherine's Monastery at the foot of Mount Sinai, which claims to have a letter from Muhammad himself guaranteeing its safety. Relations with Christians from outside the Middle East were forever strained by the arrival of the successive waves of Crusaders (from 1095 to 1291), however. The Christians living in Syria, Palestine, and Egypt were known as Christians, but the invaders were invariably referred to as Franks *(Faranj).* This distinction between local minorities who were trusted and outsiders who were not is echoed in a number of contemporary situations. The U.S. administration in the wake of the September 11, 2001, attacks, for example, distinguished between American Muslims, whom it regarded as trustworthy, and "foreign" Muslims, some of whom it regarded as representing a serious, terrorist threat. The resentment that Muslims and Christians in Europe feel toward each other, by contrast, has a different context and background. In part, it is related to a shared history of conflict (Crusades, world wars), and subsequently to subjugation and domination through colonialism by the European powers (principally France and England). In western Europe, even native-born Muslims are often denied full citizenship. In France and Germany, this is no doubt because they are predominantly members of an immigrant labor underclass; these two countries are alone in banning women from wearing the head covering in government service — something that is not an issue elsewhere in Europe, or in North America.

By all accounts the caliph 'Umar disliked being regarded as an absolute ruler and refused both title and luxury, but — or perhaps, therefore — he ruled with the greatest efficiency and success. In order effectively to administer the ever-growing empire, and to regulate salaries and taxation, 'Umar instituted the lunar Islamic calendar (year 1 of which is the Prophet's migration [Hijra] to Medina). 'Umar also leased a Byzantine church in Damascus to allow the Muslim population there to congregate for prayer, especially on Friday and on the two high holidays, the Feast of Fast-breaking (in Ramadan) and the Feast of Sacrifice (to coincide with the pilgrimage). Eventually, the Muslims took the half of the land where the church stood and built the Umayyad Mosque on the entire enclosure, with decoration by Syrian Christian artisans trained in the Byzantine tradition. Besides being an important center of religious education, the Umayyad Mosque has great symbolic significance. It houses the head of John the Baptist — the 2001 visit of John Paul II to the relic was the first time a pope had visited a mosque. It also houses the head of Muhammad's grandson Husayn (see below), and is therefore an important Shi'ite shrine (see "Shi'ites, Shi'ism," chapter 8). The Umayyad Mosque is also believed to be the site where the prophet Jesus — Muslims regard him as fully human, and do not believe he was crucified but, rather, protected by being raised up to heaven while still alive — will return to assist in defeating the Antichrist (called Dajjâl) and the forces of unbelief and darkness, before helping to usher in a time of peace and submission to God.

'Umar, in spite of his austerity, justice, and scrupulous adherence to Muhammad's example of modest and self-effacing leadership, was assassinated by one or more non-Muslim conspirators, even though he had established clear rules protecting believers in the revealed religions as dhimmîs (from dhimma, "[pact of] protection"). Dhimmîs were, to be sure, second-class citizens, as are resident aliens in some twenty-first-century countries (e.g., in the United States, where they are taxed but have no right to vote or to hold public office). 'Umar was succeeded by 'Uthmân, a caliph who reportedly promoted the interests of his kinsmen but is primarily remembered for collecting the Qur'an into a single, written, canonical codex. Curiously, for this he was both praised (since it would prevent the possibility of erring in the recitation of God's words) and vilified (he burned copies of noncanonical Qur'anic texts).

'Uthmân was assassinated by disgruntled Muslim subjects, and his successor, 'Alî, inherited a fractured polity — though the empire was financially robust, in particular thanks to the very able governor of Syria, Mu'âwiya, a kinsman of 'Uthmân. 'Alî was supported by some Muslims, especially those who claimed his primacy from the very beginning (a group that came to be know as the Shi'a, Anglicized as Shi'ites), but he was opposed by several factions, including Mu'âwiya. Their armies met in battle, but the pious 'Alî accepted Mu'âwiya's offer of arbitration over bloodshed, and Mu'âwiya thereby gained the upper hand. This opposition has a certain symmetry to it: Mu'âwiya's father, Abû-Sufyân, had been Muhammad's staunchest opponent; now his son Mu'âwiya was opposing Muhammad's son-in-law; later, Mu'âwiya's son would murder 'Alî's son (Muhammad's grandson), Husayn.

In 661, 'Alî was assassinated by a malcontent former follower (the member of a small group known as the Khârijites, or "leave-takers"). With his death, a thirty-year period described by Muslim historians as the time of the "rightly guided" *(râshidûn)* caliphs came to an end, during which all the rulers had been very close companions of Muhammad, members of his inner circle, so to speak. With 'Alî dead, Mu'âwiya claimed the caliphate and ruled for twenty years from the new capital of the Islamic empire, Damascus. In 680, he was succeeded by his son Yazîd, and thus began the first caliphal dynasty, the Umayyads (so named for an ancestor, Umayya). Mu'âwiya preserved the Byzantine civil administration; not until 697, under the later caliph 'Abd-al-Malik, did Arabic become the language of state and administration. Under the Umayyads, who ruled from 661 to 750, the Islamic empire expanded across northern Africa, and as far as Spain in the west and western China in the east. It is difficult to estimate the total Muslim population in the mid–eighth century, as most of the inhabitants in areas taken over by the Muslim rulers remained unaffected by Islam; it was, paradoxically, in the empire's interest to have subject populations remain non-Muslim, as it could collect a poll tax from non-Muslims (the *jizya*). Modern historians have remarked that certain areas welcomed the Muslims as preferable to their previous overlords, as in Roman Egypt, Persia, and Iberia. And yet, it appears that in some areas the new religion did appeal to the masses and resulted in conversions, sometimes on a large scale. This was especially true in West Africa, South Asia, and central Asia, where itinerant missionary mystics (Sufis) made Islam attractive.

Sufis were not accepted in some places, especially in certain parts of the world that were (already) predominantly Muslim, where gnostic or musical or populist or syncretic presentations of Islam were regarded as a threat to the pristine Islam of the law books. The most well-known opponent to Sufis is probably Ibn-ʿAbd-al-Wahhâb, eponym of the so-called Wahhâbi movement, influential today in Saudi Arabia. This is a puritanical, literalist brand of Islam that the Saudis can easily propagate by using their economic power (deriving principally from oil) to distribute "authorized" translations of the Qurʾan and to train scholars in seminaries and universities funded by them all over the world, and through the pilgrims who piously visit the holy cities of Mecca and Medina year-round. Though Wahhâbism is not necessarily a violent ideology, it is famously intolerant of what it regards as heterodox Muslim beliefs.

The Umayyad empire stretched from Spain to India, with a predominantly non-Arab and non-Muslim population. In 750, frustrated non-Arab Muslims rallied to the Abbasid cause and helped topple the Umayyads, who cultivated Arab and Arabian virtues and regarded non-Arab members of the Muslim polity as inferior — a form of discrimination Muhammad had specifically forbidden in his last sermon. The Abbasids (so named for Abbas, Muhammad's uncle) soon thereafter built a new capital, Baghdad, in 762, and before the end of the eighth century the "Round City" or the "City of Peace" was the envy of the world. It attracted artists and artisans, scholars and scientists, physicians and philosophers. Many of modern society's institutions have their origins in medieval Baghdad, such as the college, the hospital, the postal system, and the police force. Baghdad also had running water, observatories, philosophical societies, and law schools. It was in the latter that the principles of Islamic jurisprudence were studied. A law student, like a law student in a modern American law school, had a preparatory education first; for the medieval Muslim this typically involved memorizing the Qurʾan, learning hadiths, studying the principles of Arabic grammar, and memorizing classics from the literary tradition. In the ninth century particularly, scholarship, learning, and literary output flourished in Arabic, building on the scholarly advances of the eighth century. These included the anthologizing of the vast Arabic poetic corpus; the study of

Arabic grammar and lexicography; exegesis of the Qur'an; the sifting, collecting, and publishing of hadiths; the patronage — notably by the caliphs Hârûn al-Rashîd and al-Ma'mûn — of the translation of scientific and philosophical works from Greek and historical and political works from Middle Persian; and the development of methodological and theoretical principles in jurisprudence, literary criticism, and philosophical theology (see "Islamic Philosophy," chapter 6).

The Abbasids ruled from 750 to 1258, but from the tenth to the thirteenth century their economic success was consolidated and their resources were fragmented and spread out. As early as the ninth century, even nearby Egypt was virtually self-governing. In the tenth century, both Spain, under the Spanish Umayyad caliphate (756-1031), and Egypt, under the Shi'ite Fâtimid caliphate (909-1171), were run by rival polities actively opposed to the Abbasids. The notion that the Abbasid caliph was the head of the entire Muslim *umma* was now a fiction, and even the titular caliph's political power devolved increasingly to outlying governorates that were often autonomous and only paid lip service and tribute to the central authority in Baghdad. During the period of the Crusades, for instance, resistance was not organized by the Abbasid caliph in Baghdad, but by the Turkic rulers of Syria, and later by their Kurdish lieutenant, Saladin (Salâh-al-dîn). Saladin later defeated the Fâtimids and established himself as sultan in Cairo. The title sultan (literally, "potentate") had been in use since the advent of Turkic Muslim rule in central Asia, and would remain an important title. In the fourteenth century, Dante spared Saladin in the *Commedia,* saving him from hellfire by placing him in Limbo, and by referring to him as "the Sultan," an acknowledgment of him as an honorable ruler. In Limbo too are two important Muslim philosophers and polymaths, the Central Asian Avicenna (Ibn-Sîna, d. 1037) and the Spanish Averroës (Ibn-Rushd, d. 1198), spared because of the incalculable importance of these thinkers' works in European philosophy, medicine, and theology. Avicenna also wrote a medical textbook, the *Canon,* which was in continuous use in medical schools all over Europe until the seventeenth century. Both were also jurists, mathematicians, and scientists, and wrote on numerous other topics, as did many Muslim scholars in the Middle Ages — "renaissance" scholars before the Renaissance itself.

Becoming an intellectual of the caliber of Averroës and Avicenna was made possible by the relative ease of access to teachers, libraries, bookshops, colleges, and universities, and the sheer curiosity implicit in the intellectual milieu, which often included travel across great distances in search of knowledge *(rihla fî talab al-ʿilm)*. This is in keeping with the Qur'an's emphasis that God is worthy of worship because, among other things, "He taught humanity the use of the pen." The prominent religious scholar Jaʿfar al-Sâdiq (d. 765, great-great-grandson of ʿAlî) reportedly said that a scholar is worth a thousand worshipers.

Authority to discern and interpret the divine law for both Shiʿite and Sunni Muslims is vested in clerics. Shiʿite clerics form a hierarchy that culminates in ayatollahs, master jurists whose knowledge of the law commands allegiance from lower-level clerics (mullahs, *mujtahids*) and laypersons. Sunni clerics, by contrast, are not hierarchically organized and, in principle, are each equally entitled to develop authoritative interpretations of the law (though in practice some enjoy more prestige than others, whether through an official position or reputation in a given community) (see "Sunnis, Sunnism," chapter 9). Paradoxically, this allows anyone with authority and power to advance their brand of Islam. The threat of this possibility in the ninth century is what led jurists to close ranks and effectively ensure that only qualified jurists could interpret the law (see "Shariʿa," chapter 5). This is akin to allowing only those who hold degrees from an accredited law school and who have passed the bar exam to call themselves lawyers and practice law; it is a mechanism established to ensure that the experts control the knowledge production and the expertise. The institution where one studied law was called a *madrasa* (law college), and was residential. The first *madrasa*, the Nizâmiyya, was founded in Baghdad in 1091 by the patron Nizâm-al-Mulk, chief minister in the Seljuk Turkish empire. The word *madrasa* today is used principally to mean "Sunday school" or seminary, but its origins are medieval; during medieval times a *madrasa* dispensed higher education, not elementary or secondary education.

*   *   *

One could describe the rise and fall of several important Muslim empires in the centuries following the arrival of the Mongols on the scene in the thirteenth century, such as the Songhay empire in Niger and Burkina Faso (1468-1591), the (Shiʿite) Safavids in Persia (1501-1736), the Sultanate of Aceh in Indonesia (1496-1903), and the Ottomans in the Middle East and southeastern Europe (1293-1923) — the latter important for having ruled in Constantinople/Istanbul through to the early twentieth century and whose sultans were the last rulers to claim the title caliph. But their story is the stuff of regional, political, and economic history and international relations, not the story of Islam, the belief system. By the same token, it is a mistake to think of "the Muslim world," a term glibly deployed by many, including the Western media and academy, as a synonym for Islam. Neither journalists nor academics would refer to Europe and the Americas, say, as "the Christian world," or Israel as "the Jewish country." Similarly no one would attribute the actions or beliefs of *some* Christians to all of "Christianity," or of the Ku Klux Klan to all Americans. The assumption that an elementary school teacher in Nigeria, an actress in Canada, a shopkeeper in Pakistan, a nurse in Baghdad, an architect in Indonesia, a combatant in Guantanamo, and a criminal anywhere have a single *Muslim* view of the world is a *seriously* flawed one. Observant Muslims do, to be sure, give their religion importance; but so do observant Jews. Politically disenfranchised Muslims in Russia and Palestine do, to be sure, rail against neocolonialism, state repression, and foreign interference, but so do politically disenfranchised Christians in Russia and Palestine. The assumption that for Muslims, religious identity is more important than any other part of their identity, such as citizenship, race, gender, or class, is as flawed as assuming that this is not true of Christians or Jews.

Like everyone else, Muslims are parents, children, spouses, farmers, soldiers, writers, thinkers, activists, teachers, politicians. Like atheists and animists, Buddhists and Baptists, Jains and Jews, Muslims come in all stripes. And like the members of so many of the world's great religions, they have beliefs rooted in the words and practices of a centuries-old faith.

PART II

ORIGINS

Chapter Two

QUR'AN

Roger Allen

Term

The Arabic word *Qur'ân* (sometimes transliterated "Koran") is a derivative of a word with the meaning "to recite (orally)." The imperative of the same verb, *iqra'*, is generally acknowledged to be the opening of the first utterance revealed by God to the Prophet Muhammad, and is God's command to Muhammad that he proclaim God's revelations (Q 96:1). *Qur'ân* is thus best translated "Recitation."

This etymology is important because it underlines both the oral origins of Islam's most authoritative source and the continuing function of oral recitation and of listening to the words and sounds of the Qur'an within Muslim communities. The recording of the Qur'an textually took place after Muhammad's death, and the very process of transferring a memorized set of revelations to textual form had a profound effect on the development of the Arabic language, of a community of Muslim faithful, and of hermeneutic methodology relating to the Qur'an itself and other categories of text.

Reception

The contents of the Qur'an are the revelations of God to his Prophet Muhammad between 610 and his death in 632. Tradition has it that the first revelation came to Muhammad during a period of seclusion in a cave outside his native city of Mecca. At first he revealed the message of his revelations only to his wife, Khadîja, and other intimates. Gradually, however, he was instructed to proclaim his message — one of warning concerning the consequences of sin in this world, with examples of previous communities on whom God had wreaked vengeance — to the larger community of citizens of Mecca. At that time (the early seventh century) the city was not only a major commercial center but also the site of the Ka'ba (Arabic, *ka'ba*, "cubical structure"), a renowned shrine to various pagan deities and an associated place of pilgrimage. It is thus hardly a surprise that the import of Muhammad's message was initially not well received. As animosities worsened, he emigrated (Hijra) to the oasis of Yathrib to the northeast. The community of Yathrib thereafter developed into the city known as Medina.

At the time of Muhammad's death in 632, the revelations of both the earlier Meccan period and the subsequent Medinan one survived in the memories of Muhammad's close Companions *(Sahâba)* and followers within the small but expanding Muslim community. It was when a large number of these "carriers" *(hamala)* of the Qur'an died that it was deemed necessary to preserve the revelations in written form.

Compilation

While there are accounts of earlier compilations of the revelations, the Qur'an in book form is the result of a recording process instigated during the caliphate of 'Uthmân-ibn-'Affân (ruled 644-656). 'Uthmân expressed concern about the number of variants that, by the very nature of things, characterized the corporate memorization of a series of revelations spread over several decades.

Tradition has it that the passages of revelation were recorded from the memories of men and from a number of written fragments. The passages were categorized as belonging to the "Meccan" (pre-Hijra) or "Medinan" (post-Hijra) period and then were gathered into sections, each of which was called a sura, with a title culled from a word or phrase found within the sura. The 12th sura, for example, contains a version of the narrative of Joseph and is consequently called the Sura of Joseph (Yûsuf); the 26th contains a reference to poets and is thus known as the Sura of the Poets. The verse subdivisions are called *âyât* (sing. *âya*), literally "signs." The Qur'an opens with the "Opening [Sura]" *(Fâtiha)*, used as a prayer on numerous occasions in the life of a Muslim, but the 113 subsequent suras are arranged more or less according to length, starting with the longest, the "Sura of the Cow" *(Baqara),* which contains 286 verses, and closing with a number of very short suras that belong to the earlier Meccan period and are characterized by short verses and the use of a rhyming, rhythmic prose called *saj'.* The 114th and final sura, for example, the "Sura of Humanity" *(Nâs),* contains 6 verses in a single rhyme.

From the outset, the Qur'an, its message, and its cadences were central to the life of every Muslim, and the recitation of the text was an essential part of both corporate and individual acts of devotion. For that purpose the Qur'an was also divided into thirty subdivisions, called *juz',* so that, for example, the entire text could be read during the holy month of Ramadan, and on significant communal or private occasions.

The Qur'an was recorded in written form from memory, and it remains up till today an object of pride for Muslims to memorize and cite the text of the Qur'an. The memorization of the complete text is a project undertaken in traditional Islamic schools. The well-known autobiography of the Egyptian litterateur Tâhâ Husayn (1889-1973), translated into English as *An Egyptian Childhood* (1943), gives a clear indication of the pride that parents and community feel when a child becomes a *hâfiz* ("one who preserves," i.e., a memorizer of the Qur'an).

Language and Style

The Qur'an is the word of God transmitted to his creatures through the mediation of a "messenger" *(rasûl),* whose function it was to relay the revelations to his contemporary listeners. God speaks in the first person, issuing commands ("recite," "tell") to Muhammad the Prophet, who serves as the second-person addressee: "If my servants ask you about me, indeed I am near" (Q 2:186). Third-person discourse is used both to depict the reactions of those who are listening to the message and, when appropriate, to narrate exemplary stories of earlier prophets and peoples. Thus, in addition to direct injunctions to Muhammad to relay God's word, there are also passages that reflect the context of Muhammad's revelations. In particular, the later suras include passages that reflect the ways in which doctrinal issues would be raised within the emerging Muslim community. The usual formula is, "They will ask you concerning . . ." (e.g., the sacred month [Q 2:217], wine and gambling [Q 2:219], and menstruation [Q 2:222]), and the answer to each question is always prefaced with "Say . . ."

The Qur'an states clearly that it is "an Arabic Qur'an" (Q 12:2) and notes that every sacred revelation is presented to its people in their own language. The meaning of the utterances revealed to Muhammad is clear *(mubîn)*. From this notion there develops a major subfield of Islamic hermeneutics and criticism, the study of "clarity of expression" *(bayân)*. With the expansion of the Muslim community far beyond its original linguistic and geographic boundaries, it became necessary to explore the meaning and ramifications of these central terms regarding the discourse of the Qur'an.

As early philologists began studying and preparing commentaries on the now canonical, written text, it emerged that the revelations were couched in a style and level of language that were characteristic of the Hijaz region of the Arabian Peninsula (within which lie the two holy cities of Mecca and Medina) during the pre-Islamic period. This particular register was reserved for special occasions and was associated with the utterances of particular categories of public speakers. For that very reason, the text of the Qur'an is very explicit at several points concerning the need to differentiate the function of Muhammad as a prophet (and thus revealer of God's word) from that of other users of this same style of rhyming, rhythmic speech, namely, soothsayers and poets.

When challenged by skeptics to illustrate his prophetic function by performing a miracle, Muhammad would always point to the Qur'an. This was the "challenge" *(tahaddî),* as encountered, for example, at Q 53:24, where God says, "Let them then try and produce a recital like it!" Continuing research on the Qur'an led to the development of an enormous library of hermeneutical literature, including studies of problematic words and passages *(mushkil)* and an entire subfield of criticism devoted to the identification of its miraculous qualities (see below).

The Qur'anic Message

Central to the message of the Qur'an is Allah, the absolute and single God. The statement of faith *(shahâda)* begins with the words: "There is no god but God" (Q 37:35), and the sermon delivered by Joseph to his fellow prisoners poses the question, "Which is better: to have a number of different gods or God the One and All-powerful?" (Q 12:39). God is described in the Qur'an with numerous epithets *(al-asmâ' al-husna,* "beautiful names"); among many other attributes, He is merciful, sincere, knowing, great, and powerful. God has total power over humanity, and the charge of His message in the Qur'an is to change human behavior in this world in order to be prepared for the next. As part of the process whereby the message is communicated, God offers "signs" *(âyât)* to illustrate His judgments, mercy and forgiveness, and punishments. The fate of ancient peoples is alluded to: the ancient Arabian communities of ʿÂd and Thamûd are cited as two peoples upon whom God wreaked vengeance for their idolatry and evil practices (Q 7:65-79). The deeds of the individual in this world will be weighed in the balance on the Day of Judgment; the choice is a stark one between a gardenlike paradise of eternal bliss *(Janna)* and the excruciating torment of hellfire *(Jahannam, Nâr)*.

In the opening sura of the Qur'an, humans are to choose between following "the straight path" *(al-sirât al-mustaqîm)* and joining those who "go astray" *(dâllîn)*. Muhammad's listeners are urged to believe in the one God and in His chosen prophet. The penalties for unbelief *(kufr)* and apostasy are dire, as are those for people who make a pretense of their faith; their fate is the subject of some rather grim irony: "Give the hypocrites the good news: that they will have a gruesome punishment" (Q 4:138).

The Qur'an often resorts to the repertoire of homiletic and prophetic narratives that was presumably current in the Arabian Peninsula in the seventh century in order to provide exemplary stories of faith in adversity. Particularly during the period following the migration from Mecca to Medina, revelations refer to linkages between the revelations of the Qur'an and those of previous scriptures: "the book He has revealed to His messenger, and the book He revealed before" (Q 4:136). The status of Muhammad as continuer and "seal" of the prophetic line is made explicit in a message specifically directed at "the people of the Book" (Jews and Christians): "Now Our messenger has come to you, clarifying for you much from the Book that you have kept hidden" (Q 5:15).

We have already seen that the Qur'an includes the entire narrative of Joseph, but the lives and examples of many other exemplary figures are also mentioned, including Noah, Abraham, Solomon, and Jesus and Mary (citations regarding whom are a particular feature of the decoration in the Dome of the Rock in Jerusalem). Notable also is the inclusion of Near Eastern material such as the famous tale of the seven sleepers of Ephesus in Q 18:9-20 and, in the same sura, elements to be found in the Syriac *Alexander Legend* (Q 18:83-102), where Alexander is called Dhul-Qarnayn, "the two-horned one."

The incipient Muslim community in Medina in the period following the Prophet's migration in 622 had heard the revelations that have been briefly summarized above, but inevitably there arose questions concerning details of faith and practice and challenges to specific statements and their implications. Of the five "pillars" *(arkân)* — statement of faith, ritual-prayer, almsgiving, fasting, and pilgrimage — revelations now codify the nature of belief and religious practice for all but the pilgrimage. In response to questions from the community, guidance was provided concerning specific matters, including marriage and divorce, inheritance, dietary regulations, theft, gambling, distribution of spoils, and usury. This list of topics, when coupled with references to "hypocrites" noted above, makes it clear that some of these revelations and the regulations they impose are the consequence of particular incidents in the early life of the Muslim community in Medina. An especially notable example of this background occurs in the twenty-fourth sura, where a set of verses is clearly addressed to a group of people who have spread malicious gossip about ʿÂʾisha (d. 678), one of the Prophet Muhammad's later wives (Q 24:11-20).

While these dicta in the Qurʾan itself serve as the basic source for the belief and conduct of Muslims and also as the primary authority in the establishment of the code of Islamic law (see "Shariʿa," chapter 5), the second most important source for matters of doctrine and practice is the impeccable example of the Prophet Muhammad as recorded in the Hadith (see "Hadith and Sunna," chapter 4), the categorized corpus of reports covering the acts, statements, and tacit approvals of the Prophet during his lifetime.

The Impact of the Qurʾan

The recording of the Qurʾan in written form was an event of major importance, one that stimulated the numerous scholarly endeavors that served as the foundation for what were to become the "Islamic sciences." That intellectual milieu also fostered a system of education whose impact was felt not only throughout the ever expanding "domain of Islam" *(dâr al-Islâm)* but also far beyond it. Initial studies of the Qurʾan needed to focus on the text itself: its language and syntactic structures (including such basics as the conventions of the alphabet) and the authenticity of the recorded segments. That focus led in turn to research on the genealogy of individuals and tribal groups and to the compilation of linguistic precedents, particularly in the form of an elaborate oral corpus of poetry from the pre-Islamic era. From the analysis of the Qurʾan's content emerged compilations of principles of belief, codifications of jurisprudence, and studies in theology. The urgent need to sift through the vast collection of hadith reports of the Prophet's behavior and recorded statements led to the development of principles of textual analysis and criticism. The study of these and other subfields became the focus of a system of education whereby learning (*'ilm;* whence *'âlim,* "knowing [scholar]," "learned [indvidual]"; pl. *'ulamâ')* became the path to religious authority as it was passed on from one generation to the next.

As methods of critical analysis were applied to various types of text, the unique nature of the Qur'an itself, implicit in the challenge that had been posed by Muhammad to replicate its qualities, was subsumed under the heading of "the Qur'an's inimitability" *(i'jâz al-Qur'ân).* Several prominent figures in Arabic literature wrote texts in imitation of the Qur'an's style; one is a poet renowned as al-Mutanabbî, "the would-be Prophet" (d. 965), for doing so, while al-Bâqillânî (d. 1013) compares the stylistic and moral message of the Qur'an with pre-Islamic poetry in order to prove the superiority of the former. In contemporary literature, poets such as Amal Dunqul (d. 1983), Muhammad 'Afîfî Matar (b. 1935), and Adûnîs ('Alî Ahmad Sa'îd, b. 1930), and novelists such as Naguib Mahfouz (d. 2006) and Driss Chraïbi (b. 1926), quote, adapt, and rework the Qur'an to powerful effect.

The Qur'an remains an indivisible part of the history of the Arabic language and its texts and of the Muslim peoples of the world. The advent of modern media means that the Qur'an's presence in the oral dimension is even more powerful than before. Whether it is through the broadcast on television of the five daily prayers and Friday congregational prayer, the availability in digitized form of the sacred text, the amplified sound of the muezzin *(mu'adhdhin)* summoning the faithful to prayer — to be heard in all Muslim communities — or its accessibility through cell phone and personal computer, and the widespread use of audio recordings, the Qur'an continues to be prevalent in the daily life of large segments of the world's population.

Chapter Three

MUHAMMAD

Tahera Qutbuddin

Early Life in Mecca

Muhammad (d. 632), the "Messenger of God," was born in 570 in the city of Mecca, located in the heart of the Arabian Peninsula. Flanked by two powerful empires — the Sassanids in Persia and the Byzantines in Syria-Palestine — the inhabitants of the peninsula led camel caravans through its arid wastes to trade in those lands. Arabian society was tribal, its security maintained through alliances among the tribes and by mutual threat of blood revenge. Although a few Jewish and Christian tribes lived in parts of the peninsula and in neighboring Syria and Mesopotamia, most of the inhabitants of the region worshiped pagan deities such as Lât, 'Uzza, and Manât. Moreover, the Arabs were largely nomadic; the majority of the tribes migrated with the seasons from one watering place to the next, and a few lived in towns that were settled next to oases, or around shrines built near water springs and dedicated to various deities. Mecca was one of these settled towns, and an important center of commerce and religion. It was home to the Ka'ba, a cubical structure built, according to Islamic belief, as the House of God *(Bayt Allâh)* by the Prophet Adam and later rebuilt by the Prophet Abraham, and converted over time into a pagan shrine. Large numbers of Arabs came to Mecca during the annual pilgrimage season to circumambulate the shrine, and also during the yearly fair at nearby 'Ukâz for trade and cultural exchange.

Mecca's population included the influential tribe of Quraysh, descended according to Muslim tradition from Abraham through his son Ishmael. Muhammad was born into one of its preeminent clans, the Banû Hâshim, who were the guardians of the Ka'ba. Orphaned at a tender age — his father 'Abdallah died around the time he was born, and his mother Âmina passed away when he was six — Muhammad was raised by his paternal grandfather, 'Abd-al-Muttalib, until he was eight, and then by his paternal uncle, Abû-Tâlib. Muhammad became known at an early age for his integrity and honesty, and the Meccans nicknamed him "the Trustworthy One" *(al-Amîn)*.

In his youth, Muhammad often traveled to Syria with Abû-Tâlib to trade, and on one of these journeys a wealthy Meccan widow named Khadîja employed him as her commercial agent. Captivated by his uprightness and sagacity, she proposed to him and they were married. Muhammad was then twenty-five, Khadîja about forty. He and Khadîja had two sons, Qâsim and 'Abdallah, nicknamed Tayyib ("the Good") and Tâhir ("the Pure"), who both died in infancy, and four daughters, Zaynab, Ruqayya, Umm-Kulthûm, and Fâtima, who all survived into adulthood. After Khadîja's death and his subsequent remarriages, Muhammad would have just one more child, a son named Ibrâhîm (Abraham) who also died in infancy. Muhammad's line was destined to continue solely through the progeny of Fâtima and her husband 'Alî (the son of Abû-Tâlib), a line that would become the locus for the Shi'ite doctrine of the imamate (see "Shi'ites, Shi'ism," chapter 8).

Revelation, Prophecy, and the Birth of Islam

Muhammad was a man given to deep thought, and he regularly spent quiet hours meditating in a cave on Mount Hira outside Mecca. According to Muslim historians, it was here in 610 at the age of forty that he first received God's message, when the archangel Gabriel came to him and instructed, "Recite in the name of your Lord, who created human beings from a blood clot" (Q 96:1-2). This revealed "recitation" *(Qur'ân)* became the first of many that together — in 6,236 verses *(âyât)* and 114 chapters (suras) of varying lengths — would constitute the scripture of Islam, the Qur'an (see "Qur'an," chapter 2).

The early suras laid out some of the fundamentals of Islam. Among the first revelations was the "Sura of Sincerity" *(Ikhlâs, Q 112:1-4)*:

In the Name of God, Ever Compassionate, Full of Compassion,
Say: He is God, Matchless; God, Ceaseless;
Not begetting and Not begotten; Without a single partner, Peerless.

With its four pithy verses proclaiming God's unity, this sura comprised the core doctrine of Islam. Another was the "Sura of Praise" *(Hamd),* also called "The Opening" *(Fâtiha,* Q 1:1-7):

> *In the Name of God, Ever Compassionate, Full of Compassion,*
> Praise to the Lord of all Creation, Ever Compassionate, Full of
> Compassion, Sovereign of The Day of Determination: You alone do
> we worship, and You alone do we ask for aid. Guide us on the
> straight path, The path of those you favor, not of those who earn
> Your wrath, nor of those in deviation.

With its seven short verses of prayer, this sura became a basic invocation in Islam, in status not unlike the Lord's Prayer in Christianity.

Summoned to God's service, Muhammad began calling others to the worship of the one God. He professed the creed that was to become the key testimony *(shahâda)* of Islam: "There is no god but God." At first he approached his wife Khadîja, who accepted Islam, then his young cousin and ward 'Ali. Then, one by one, he brought aboard several members of his clan and other members and affiliates of the Quraysh tribe, including Abû-Bakr and 'Umar (who later became leaders), until the Muslims numbered a few dozen. Muhammad then began preaching openly to his people and also to the pilgrims who visited Mecca, warning of the transitory nature of this world and the imminence of the hereafter. Emphasizing accountability for one's actions, the early Meccan revelations (and Muhammad's own speeches) painted vivid pictures of the rewards and punishments of one's deeds, embodied in the pleasures of paradise and the tortures of hellfire. They condemned many of the immoral social practices of pagan Arabia such as female infanticide, usury, and blood revenge.

The Meccans were not pleased with Muhammad's activities. Fearing his growing influence and the possible political consequences of the spread of Islam, they began to starve and beat many of the weaker members of the new religion. In 615, Muhammad had to send these followers away for their own safety under the leadership of his cousin Ja'far to seek refuge with the Christian ruler of Abyssinia (modern-day Ethiopia in Africa, across the Red Sea from Arabia). In 616, two powerful clans of the Quraysh (Makhzûm and 'Abd-Shams/Umayya) instituted a social boycott prohibiting interaction with Muhammad's Hâshim clan. Except for Muhammad's paternal uncle Abû-Lahab, who vehemently opposed him, the Hâshimites had by and large supported Muhammad. Abû-Tâlib, their chief, had offered him the full protection of the clan; now they lived in dire straits until the boycott ended three years later in 619.

It is from Mecca that Muhammad is believed to have made the Night Journey *(Isrâ')* to the holy land of Jerusalem and to have led all the earlier prophets in congregational prayer there. From Jerusalem, he is said to have attained ascension *(Mi'râj)* to the seven heavens, until he "drew close and yet closer, till he was at a distance of a bow's length or even closer" to God (Q 53:9). Some Muslims regard this as a miraculous physical journey; others deem it to have been a spiritual experience. During the ascension Muhammad received instructions from God to make obligatory the five daily ritual-prayers *(salât)*. Indeed, it is during Muhammad's years of preaching in Mecca that he instituted many of the worship rites that would become part of the mandatory "pillars" of Islam.

When Abû-Tâlib and Khadîja both died in 619, the Quraysh stepped up their offensive against Muhammad and the Muslims. Abû-Lahab had become the new Hâshimite chief, and he withdrew the clan's protection from Muhammad, leaving him open to attacks on his very life. Continued residence in Mecca became not only difficult, but dangerous, so Muhammad began looking for a more favorable location for his mission. He journeyed to the neighboring shrine city of Tâ'if, but found its inhabitants from the powerful Thaqîf tribe unwelcoming. Two years later during the 621 pilgrimage season in Mecca, a small delegation from the flourishing northern agricultural settlement of Yathrib came to Muhammad at the hill of 'Aqaba outside Mecca. They accepted Islam and pledged allegiance to Muhammad. Early the following year, in 622, they came again in greater numbers and reached a formal agreement, whereby Muhammad would come to Yathrib as its chief and his followers would enter into its protection. Soon thereafter Muhammad's followers in Mecca began migrating to Yathrib in small groups; they came to be known as the "Emigrants" *(Muhâjirûn)*, and along with the Muslims of Medina who gave succor to them, known as the "Helpers" *(Ansâr)*, they would be honored by later Muslims for their sincere service to Islam. They would also be known as the Companions *(Sahâba)* of Muhammad. In the spring of that year, Muhammad himself migrated to Yathrib, which from then on was called Madînat al-Nabi, the "City of the Prophet," shortened to Medina. The year of his migration was later marked as year 1 of the lunar Islamic calendar, called the Hijri calendar, from the word *Hijra*, "the Migration."

The Making of the Muslim Community in Medina

Arriving in Medina in 622, Muhammad embarked upon a new phase; in addition to his role as the Prophet of Islam, he became the political and military head of the nascent Muslim community *(umma)*. The Constitution of Medina — a document preserved by an early historian — lays out in some detail the tribal-religious makeup and political composition of the Medinan community at the time of the Prophet's migration there. Large numbers from both of Medina's pagan tribes of Aws and Khazraj had already converted to Islam when Muhammad arrived, and this continued until both groups were almost entirely Muslim. The three Medinan Jewish tribes of Nadîr, Qurayza, and Qaynuqa' did not convert, but they accepted Muhammad as their political leader and entered into an alliance with the Muslims to defend and protect one another. The Constitution of Medina named "God and His Prophet Muhammad" final arbiter for all the residents of Medina, and made it incumbent upon them to obey Muhammad.

Even as the new community was being set up in Medina, the discord between the Muslims and the Meccans was escalating. Small armed skirmishes between them had begun to take place almost immediately following the migration, preludes to several larger, pitched battles. In 624, a Meccan caravan on its way home from Syria learned of Muhammad's plans to attack it and called up a large military force to engage the much smaller group of three hundred Muslims. In the Battle of Badr (the site of some wells a short distance from Medina), the pagan force was roundly defeated by the Muslims; news of their victory over the powerful Meccans immediately resonated throughout the peninsula, establishing Muhammad as a force to be reckoned with. The Meccans came back to fight the Muslims again in 625 at the Battle of Uhud (the name of a hill just outside Medina), and again in 627 at the Battle of Khandaq (literally "trench," named for the trench the Muslims dug around their city to prevent the Meccans and their allies from entering). There were ups and downs for both sides, but overall, the power of the Meccan Quraysh was clearly slipping.

Meanwhile, conflicts had erupted internally in Medina between the Muslims and the local Jewish tribes. The Constitution of Medina had made Jews equal to Muslims in exchange for political loyalty, but during the Battles of Badr and Uhud, leaders of the Jewish tribes collaborated secretly with the Quraysh to overthrow Muhammad. Consequently in 624 and 625, Muhammad expelled the Qaynuqa' and Nadîr with their families and possessions from Medina. After the Battle of Khandaq in 627, the remaining Jewish tribe was accused of plotting with the Meccans against Muhammad's life. An arbiter was selected jointly by the Muslims and the Jews who passed an execution order against the male members of the Qurayza. Also in the Battle of Khandaq, the Jews of Khaybar (an oasis northwest of Medina that housed large numbers of the erstwhile Medinan Nadîr tribe members) had incited neighboring tribes to join the Meccan confederation against Muhammad. In 628, Muhammad fought and defeated them in the Battle of Khaybar. (See "Islam and Judaism," chapter 13.)

On the Meccan front, Muhammad had signed the Treaty of Hudaybiyya with the Quraysh in 628 agreeing to cease hostilities. But soon thereafter, the Meccans broke the treaty by aiding a third party against a Muslim tribe, and Muhammad declared a resumption of warfare. In the interim of peace, Muhammad had concentrated on proselytizing among the tribes, and by this time about ten thousand peninsula Arabs had converted to Islam. In 630, Muhammad entered Mecca in triumph with a huge army, and took control of the city without bloodshed. He granted amnesty to his erstwhile enemies, and the Quraysh accepted Islam en masse. With the conquest of Mecca, Muhammad's authority in the peninsula became supreme. In the next year, 631, called the Year of the Delegations, tribes from all over the peninsula sent deputations to declare their acceptance of Muhammad as spiritual prophet and political leader. By the end of that year, almost all of Arabia pledged allegiance to Muhammad.

Over the years in Medina, Muhammad had continued to receive revelations that elaborated Islamic doctrine and practice, and were underwritten by a call for community-oriented living and socioeconomic justice. They addressed in detail some of the ritual and legal issues that arose in the early Muslim society, combining spirituality with humane ideals. In the second year of the Hijra came the stipulation of fasting *(sawm)* — dawn-to-dusk abstention, annually during the ninth Muslim month of Ramadan, from all food, drink, and sexual activity. A little later, the Medinan revelations instituted a compulsory yearly alms-tax on wealth *(zakât)* to be collected from all who had the means and distributed among the poor; it was to be considered part of the rites of worship. The suras revealed at this time also set down laws governing civic issues such as marriage and inheritance, and directives dealing with crimes such as stealing and murder. Additionally, these suras dwelt in great detail upon the earlier prophets and their missions, including Moses (the prophet mentioned most in the Qur'an) and Jesus, as well as most biblical prophets and some Arabian ones; they presented Muhammad as the current, the last, and the greatest incumbent of divine messengerhood — the "seal of the prophets" *(khâtam al-anbiyâ')*. In both their recounting of these issues and independently of them, the Medinan suras continued to encourage Muslims to lead pious lives and be good human beings. In social areas this included caring for orphans, encouraging widow remarriage, and ensuring the well-being of the disadvantaged members of society; in ethical matters, speaking truth, being trustworthy in one's dealings, and nurturing one's fellows; in spiritual issues, establishing regular prayer, and fasting. All these teachings were underpinned by a consistent injunction to God-fearing piety *(taqwa)*.

In 631, Muhammad led the annual pilgrimage *(hajj)* to the Ka'ba in Mecca; this too was presented as another compulsory duty in Islam, to be performed by every able Muslim man and woman at least once in his or her lifetime. By bringing Muslims regardless of position, wealth, or gender to stand together in the sight of God, the pilgrimage, in addition to its spiritual function, had a social utility. Muhammad encouraged all the Muslims of the Arabian Peninsula to attend the pilgrimage with him, indicating that this first one of his would also be his last, and large numbers flocked to Mecca. On the return journey, he stopped at the springs of Ghadir Khumm, where, according to the Shi'ites, he publicly appointed 'Alî his successor. According to the Sunnis, Muhammad's speech at Khumm extolled 'Alî but had no succession context; they believe the Prophet died without appointing an heir. (See "Sunnis, Sunnism," chapter 9, and "Islamic Government," chapter 11.)

Back in Medina, Muhammad fell ill, and soon thereafter, in 632, at sixty-three years of age, he passed away. In just twenty-three years — thirteen in Mecca and ten in Medina — he had transformed Arabia from an inward-looking, fractured, largely pagan society into a dynamic community of believers united by their faith in the monotheistic teachings of Islam.

Muhammad in Muslim Piety and Literature

Muhammad is a constant presence in the lives of Muslims, as beloved guide and source of comfort in this world, and as intercessor for forgiveness of sins in the next. The Qur'an calls him the embodiment of God's "mercy for all the worlds" *(rahma lil-'âlamîn,* Q 21:107), and Muslims earnestly solicit his benevolence. Moreover, they invoke him in their personal lives as well as their public ones, in private contemplation and prayer, and in the performance of a myriad of mundane activities. Although there are few images of Muhammad (visual representation is considered reprehensible by many Muslims lest it lead to worship of icons and idols), Muslims laud and quote the Prophet regularly in poetry, Qur'anic exegesis, and theological treatises, and they reference him in their legal activities as well as their spiritual teaching and religious ritual. The historical record of his deeds and words — known collectively as the Prophet's Sunna (tradition), or the Hadith, and individually as hadiths (traditions) — is critically important for Muslims; scholars and laypeople alike consistently cite the Prophetic hadiths alongside the Qur'an as a font of inspiration and a source of guidance. (See "Hadith and Sunna," chapter 4.)

Muslims regard Muhammad as the model of the perfect human being, and the paradigmatic exemplar par excellence. Having reached the pinnacle of human goodness, he is the one to be emulated in all aspects of a Muslim's life. The Qur'an enjoins Muslims to follow his example, saying, "You will find in the Messenger of God a righteous model" (Q 33:21); it emphasizes his high character in the verse "Indeed, you [O Muhammad] possess excellent moral principles" (Q 68:4). Muslim mystics such as Ibn-'Arabî (d. 1240) and Jalâl-al-dîn Rûmî (d. 1273) consider Muhammad one of the highest links in the initiate's spiritual chain to God, the saints themselves being illuminated by the "Muhammadan light" (see "Sufism," chapter 7). Philosophers such as Ibn-Sîna (Avicenna, d. 1037) deem him a perfect intellectual who was also a perfect communicator, one who received the highest truths and was able to convey them to mankind (see "Islamic Philosophy," chapter 6). And Shi'ites such as Mu'ayyad Shîrâzî (d. 1078) find in him both the embodiment of an angelic being and the zenith of humanity in the perfect fruition of the faculty of reason.

Muhammad has been the subject of a large body of Islamic literature, in languages ranging from Arabic, Persian, Turkish, and Urdu to Swahili, Malay, Hausa, and English; in historical writings and biographies of the Prophet *(sîra);* and in treatises on specialized topics such as the Prophet's Night Journey to Jerusalem and ascent to heaven. One of the most prominent genres in Muhammad-related Muslim literature is praise poetry *(na't* and *madh)*. The tradition began in the Prophet's lifetime itself, with Hassân-ibn-Thâbit writing verses praising Muhammad and defending him against the invective of the Meccan poets, and the newly converted Ka'b-ibn-Zuhayr addressing a panegyric to him after the conquest of Mecca called the "Ode of the Mantle" *(Qasîdat al-Burda)*. Poetry composed in praise of the Prophet developed yet further in medieval times to become a prominent literary genre. The high point of the tradition came in the form of the Egyptian Berber poet al-Busîri's (d. ca. 1296) 160-line Arabic encomium of the same name as Ka'b's "Ode of the Mantle." Al-Busîri's ode attracted numerous commentaries and adaptations, and was imitated time and again across different periods, places, and languages. In South Asia, the tradition was emulated with vigor, and Âzâd Bilgrâmî (d. 1785), author of lyrical Arabic poems, came to be likened to Muhammad's own panegyrist.

Muhammad is known by many names and titles, which reflect his standing in the eyes of the Muslims and their relationship to him. Most commonly, he is called the Prophet *(nabî)* and the Messenger of God *(rasûl Allah* in Arabic, *payghambar* in Persian, Turkish, and Urdu). He is also described by the Qur'anic epithets "warner" *(nadhîr),* "bringer of good tidings" *(bashîr),* "witness" *(shâhid),* "shining lamp" *(sirâj munîr),* "one who summons" (others to God) *(dâ'î),* and *ummî* (interpreted by some to mean "unlettered," and thus a pure vessel for God's message, and by others to be "of a community, *umma").* He is further known by the names Ahmad (a variation of Muhammad, literally "praiseworthy"), Mustafa and Mukhtar (both meaning "the chosen one"), and Tâhâ and Yâsîn (two names for him in the Qur'an). The name Muhammad — along with its derivatives Ahmad, Mahmûd, and Hamada in Arabic, and its renditions into other languages as Mehmet, Mamadou, and Amadou — is said to be the most common given name in the world.

Muhammad is credited by Muslims with the performance of miracles *(mu'jiza).* Many say his greatest miracle is the Qur'an and its divine guidance. But they also relate more physical wonders, particularly at his birth, such as a large crack appearing suddenly in the grand hall of the Persian monarch Chosroes, signaling the end of the mighty Persian Empire at his hands; later, a cloud continuously moved over Muhammad to give him shade, protecting him from the hot desert sun. One of the most famous miracles attributed to Muhammad is the splitting of the moon at his behest, validating him as God's messenger, one whom the very elements obey. These miracles are prominent themes in Muslim literary works.

For most Muslims, a visit *(ziyâra)* to Muhammad's tomb at Medina is a dearly beloved aspiration, and they consider it a source of healing *(shifâ')* and grace *(baraka).* Indeed, a visit to the Prophet's earthly resting place — to perform the ritual prayer in his mosque and pay respects at his grave — is deemed a duty alongside the required pilgrimage to Mecca.

The Qur'an enjoins Muslims to invoke peace and blessings *(salawât)* upon the Prophet, in the verse: "Verily, God and His angels invoke bless-ings upon the Prophet. O you who believe, you too invoke blessings upon him and send greeting of peace" (Q 33:56). The most commonly used form of the invocation is "O God, shower blessings and peace upon Muhammad and his progeny," and the Sunnis (and sometimes the Shi'ites too) add "and upon his Companions." Muslims recite this blessings formula alongside their own individual and collective prayers, with religious ritual; at the opening and closing of speeches, sermons, and treatises on religious and secular topics; and often apart from any specific occasion. They also in-voke blessings upon Muhammad whenever they mention his name.

The way Muslims revere Muhammad is different from the way Chris-tians revere Christ. For Christians, Jesus is the Son of God, part of the Holy Trinity, and himself divine. For Muslims, Muhammad (like Jesus before him) is a creature of God, not a deity; God transcendent is indivisible and "one . . . not begetting and not begotten." Muslims do not worship Muham-mad; they are followers of Muhammad inasmuch as they accept his mes-sage. But in the manner detailed above, Muhammad is a constant presence in their lives. They invoke him constantly as guide and model, as interces-sor and friend, and as the prophet who taught them to lead a righteous life and to worship the one true God. They reaffirm his divine messengerhood — and their deep personal bond with him — in each of their five daily rit-ual prayers, with the muezzin's chanted call that echoes the key Islamic doctrine cited earlier: "I bear witness that there is no god but God. I bear witness that Muhammad is the Messenger of God."

Chapter Four

HADITH AND SUNNA

Scott C. Lucas

Sunna, an ancient Arabic term meaning "custom," or "way," emerged as a central normative concept for Muslims within the first two centuries of Islam, and soon came to refer to the example or exemplary practice of the Prophet Muhammad (d. 632). Religious scholars consequently went to great lengths to collect reports of Muhammad's actions, statements, and practices that received his tacit approval. These reports are collectively known as the Hadith, and are individually called hadiths, from the Arabic term meaning "speech" or "report." Each individual hadith consists of the text of a report (the *matn*) and the names of the succession of individuals, or "chain of transmitters/authorities" (the *isnâd*), who transmitted the report. For Sunnis, every chain of transmitters must ideally go back to the Prophet through one of his Companions *(Sahâba)*.

By the early ninth century, the collection and study of hadiths were evolving into an organized discipline that both served the formulation of legal norms and addressed pietistic concerns. A small number of scholars began to arrange hadiths into collections organized either according to the topics treated or according to the Companions of Muhammad who first reported them; the earliest collections appear to have included many non-Prophetic hadiths as well, that is, reports of the opinions of Muhammad's Companions and their successors. Six such hadith collections, consisting exclusively of Prophetic hadiths, achieved canonical status by the eleventh or twelfth century; two of them, those of al-Bukhâri (d. 870) and of Muslim (d. 875), have long been recognized by Sunni Muslims as the most authentic collections of prophetic Sunna, hence their designation as *Sahîh* collections, literally "authentic" or "authenticated." Together with four other compendia, the so-called Six Collections constitute the authoritative corpus of Sunni hadiths (though, to be sure, numerous noncanonical hadith collections from the ninth and tenth centuries also survive).

The Sunna of the Prophet Muhammad, as recorded in the hadith collections, exerted a major impact on all aspects of Islam, legal, ethical, theological, and mystical. Al-Shâfi'i (d. 820) is regarded as the preeminent champion of the legal authority of Hadith among the famous early jurists, although Mâlik-ibn-Anas (d. ca. 795) and Ahmad-ibn-Hanbal (d. 855), two jurists of comparable stature, were generally held to be better Hadith scholars per se. Later Sunni legal theorists based their belief in the trustworthiness of prophetic Sunna in the principle that Muhammad was "protected from sin" *(ma'sûm)*, but they disagreed about which of Muhammad's actions and pronouncements had to be considered obligatory or binding on other Muslims, which were recommended, and which were merely acceptable. They also disagreed on whether Muhammad's actions took precedence over his statements in those cases where a contradiction between the two was reported.

Just as Sunni Muslims have a treasured corpus of Prophetic Sunna, so too do Shi'ite Muslims. The largest group of Shi'ites, known as the "Twelvers" (for the number of Imams they acknowledge), has its own collections, four of which are considered canonical. Twelver Shi'ite hadiths (also called *akhbâr*) differ structurally from Sunni hadiths because of the core Twelver belief that all twelve Imams were, like the Prophet, "protected from sin"; consequently, the chains of transmitters of their hadiths must trace back only to *one* of the first eleven Imams, whereas, as we noted above, for Sunnis every chain of transmitters must go back to the Prophet. Thus, while books on Twelver Shi'ite legal theory share with their Sunni counterparts a common set of discussions on the Sunna, most of the Shi'ite Hadith does not meet the minimal requirements for authenticity in the eyes of Sunni scholars, since the chains of transmitters rarely go back to Muhammad in an uninterrupted fashion. Similarly, Shi'ite scholars dismiss most Sunni hadiths as inauthentic because of a general rejection of the trustworthiness of many of the Companions of the Prophet and other early transmitters featuring in Sunni chains of transmitters, and because of the Shi'ite belief that only the Imams and their students preserve reliable information about Qur'anic and Prophetic teachings.

Western scholarship on Sunna has revolved overwhelmingly around the question of whether the vast corpus of Sunni hadiths is authentic.

Western scholars have generally taken a pessimistic view of hadiths as accurate reports of Prophetic practice, although there is much agreement that this material is useful as a source for the history of the first century of Islam. Modern Muslim scholars (and reformers) have also scrutinized the corpus of hadiths for authenticity, especially in connection with such questions as Prophetic and temporal authority. Much fruitful research remains to be done on the development and influence of Hadith literature from the ninth century to the present, especially since one of the most popular books among Muslims today is *The Gardens of the Righteous,* a thirteenth-century collection of hadiths by the Sunni scholar al-Nawawî (d. 1277), and because of the continued importance of the Prophetic example to Muslims of all denominations.

PART III

DOCTRINE

Chapter Five

SHARI'A

Aron Zysow

Term

Sharî'a (also *shar'*) refers to the successive religions revealed by God to his messengers *(rusul,* sing. *rasûl),* culminating in the final messenger, Muhammad (d. 632), as well as more narrowly their practical ordinances, both taken as a whole and taken individually. It is in the latter sense of a revealed religious law that Shari'a came to mean Islamic law.

For most Muslims Islam is a legalistic religion, and Muslims understand the earlier revealed religions of Judaism and Christianity as similarly legalistic. Whereas the theological doctrines of Islam corroborate and clarify the theological truths of the earlier revelations, the religious law of Islam abrogates the divinely ordained laws that preceded it. It is disputed among Muslim scholars whether this abrogation *(naskh)* is total or whether some elements of the earlier laws continue to bind Muslims *(shar' man qablana shar' lana,* "the law of those before us is law for us"). Muslims commonly view the changes in law introduced by Islam as tending in the direction of freedom from burdensome restrictions (see Q 7:157) and accordingly speak of Islam as *dîn al-yusr,* "the religion of ease." The account of the Shari'a given below focuses on developments within Sunni Islam (see "Sunnis, Sunnism," chapter 9), the tradition of the great majority of Muslims (for Shi'ite law, see "Shi'ites, Shi'ism," chapter 8).

The Sources of Law

There is widespread agreement among Sunni jurists that Islamic law has four primary sources. The first in priority is the Qur'an, the word of God revealed to Muhammad. Only a relatively small proportion, traditionally 500, of the 6,236 verses of the Qur'an deals with legal topics, but these 500 include the fundamentals of ritual-prayer *(salât),* the fast of Ramadan *(sawm),* the alms-tax on wealth *(zakât),* the pilgrimage *(hajj),* and basic elements of contract, marriage, divorce, inheritance, the law of war, and criminal law. The authenticity of the Qur'anic text is regarded as beyond question, based as it is upon widespread unbroken transmission from generation to generation (the doctrine of *tawâtur,* "concurrence"). There is, in fact, very substantial uniformity in the received Qur'anic text, uniformity that is generally attributed to the promulgation by the caliph 'Uthmân (d. 656) of an official text of the Qur'an, the most significant governmental act by far in the entire history of Islamic law. Agreement on the text of the Qur'an does not, however, preclude widespread disagreement on its interpretation.

The second revealed source of Islamic law is the Sunna (see "Hadith and Sunna," chapter 4), or precedent of Muhammad, which encompasses his statements, actions, and tacit approval of the statements and actions of others. The great majority of jurists regard the Sunna as of fully equal authority with the Qur'an on all matters. Thus the Sunna can govern the interpretation of the Qur'an or even abrogate a prior inconsistent Qur'anic provision. In most cases, however, the Sunna is known by hadith reports that, unlike the Qur'an, were never promulgated in an official collection, and the reliability of many of these reports has long been a topic of dispute. The developments in the specialist study of such reports, culminating among Sunnis in the highly regarded collections of al-Bukhâri (d. 870) and Muslim-ibn-al-Hajjâj (d. 875), came after the formative period of Sunni law, and in any case these and similar collections did not definitively resolve the question of authenticity.

The third source of law is the consensus *(ijmâ')* of the expert jurists *(mujtahid*s, see below). The theory of consensus holds that if the expert jurists alive at a particular time agree on the answer to a legal question, their agreement serves to identify the one correct opinion and binds all subsequent Muslims. The theory of consensus does not, however, guarantee that any such agreement will take place, and in fact the instances of consensus are few in relation to the many issues that remain disputed.

The fourth source is analogy *(qiyâs)*, which provides for the generalization of a specific provision of the revealed law to encompass cases not expressly within its terms. The medieval Muslim jurists extensively developed the theory of analogy, and several varieties of analogy were distinguished. The form of analogy most widely accepted does not proceed directly from case to case but seeks to identify the element, the so-called cause *('illa)*, in the case addressed by revelation that accounts for how it has been regulated. Once this element is identified, the same regulation can be extended to any and all cases in which the same causal element is found. For example, on the assumption that the meaning of *khamr* is grape wine, the drinking of which is prohibited by the Qur'an (Q 5:90), jurists who determine that grape wine was prohibited because of its power to intoxicate can appeal to analogy in extending this prohibition to all other intoxicants.

Ijtihâd and the Schools of Legal Thought

Islamic tradition traces the main institutions of Islamic law back to the time of Muhammad and his immediate followers, notably his Companions *(Sahâba)*, and portrays Muhammad as appointing judges and other officials to administer the law of the Qur'an and Sunna. Most important, Muhammad ordained recourse to *ijtihâd* (literally "exertion," here legal reasoning in the broadest sense) in the absence of clear guidance in the Qur'an and Sunna, and it is *ijtihâd* that gave rise to the enormous development of Islamic law. Because the legal opinions arrived at by *ijtihâd* are generally admitted to be no more than probably correct, Islamic law tolerates an enormous range of disagreement *(ikhtilâf)*. There is equally diverse opinion on what to make of this ubiquitous disagreement. Many regard it as a mercy from God, in that it offers Muslims a range of valid solutions to their everyday legal problems. At the same time, many continue to believe that only one of the various discordant opinions correctly reflects God's law, although precisely which one may be unknowable. A distinction is sometimes made between the Shari'a, the law actually ordained by God, and the *fiqh* (understanding) of that law on the part of the legal scholars *(faqihs)*. Accordingly, *fiqh* is the common term for the law developed by the jurists.

Qualifying as a *mujtahid* (one capable of engaging in *ijtihâd*) is essentially a question of learning and ability and thus potentially open to all Muslims. Until recently, however, most Sunni Muslims have held that the "gate of *ijtihâd* was closed," that is, that *mujtahids* of the highest rank were not to be found after the early centuries of Islam. These Muslims were content with following (*taqlîd,* literally, "investing with authority") the legal opinions of one or another of four early *mujtahids* whose teachings were continuously studied and elaborated by successive generations of jurists in scholarly traditions known as schools of legal thought or jurisprudence *(madhhabs).* The four extant Sunni schools of jurisprudence — the Hanafîs, Mâlikîs, Shâfi'îs, and Hanbalîs — follow the teachings of Abû-Hanîfa (d. 767), Mâlik-ibn-Anas (d. 795), al-Shâfi'î (d. 820), and Ahmad-ibn-Hanbal (d. 855) (or their disciples), respectively, and regard each other as mutually orthodox. The present situation among Twelver Shi'ites is significantly different, in that ordinarily adherence to the teachings of a living *mujtahid* is required, a principle that accounts for the emergence at any given time of a small number of prominent grand ayatollahs (*âyat Allah,* literally "sign of God), who serve as loci *(marja's)* for their followers.

In the premodern period, training in the law developed by the schools of legal thought was an integral part of a comprehensive Islamic education and served as preparation for a variety of careers but not typically that of professional advocate, a figure rare in traditional Muslim courts. The influence of the different legal schools waxed and waned for a variety of personal and political reasons, and change of affiliation by individuals from one legal school to another was possible. In some regions and for relatively long periods of time, a single legal school could come to enjoy a virtual monopoly of influence, for example, the Mâlikî school in Islamic Spain and North Africa, the Hanafî school in Mughal India (1526-1720) and the Ottoman Empire (1290-1924), the Shâfi'î school in Indonesia, and the Twelver Shi'ite school in Iran from the time of the Safavids (1501-1736).

Most of the legal writing produced by the jurists of the various legal schools over the centuries, much still in manuscript, can be classified as either legal theory (*usûl al-fiqh,* "the roots of understanding") or substantive law (*furû' al-fiqh,* "the branches of understanding"). Legal theory identifies the sources of the law, guides the interpretation of the textual sources, and defines the authority of the opinions arrived at by *ijtihâd.*

The Substantive Law

The substantive law represents the rules of law that result from the application of *ijtihâd* to the sources. These are typically presented in more or less comprehensive treatises, but also in collections of legal opinions (*fatâwa,* sing. *fatwa)* by respondents (the muftis), both official and unofficial, to inquiries on a wide range of questions. The substantive law of Islam operates with a number of general classifications. The most basic is the classification of all human acts under one of five categories: obligatory *(wâjib)*, recommended *(mandûb)*, disapproved *(makrûh)*, permitted *(mubâh)*, or prohibited *(harâm)*. The first four collectively constitute the domain of the licit *(halâl)*. Marriage under normal circumstances, to take just one example, is commonly categorized as recommended.

A second broad classification is between the claims of God *(huqûq Allah)* and those of humans *(huqûq al-âdamiyyîn)*. As distinguished from the claims of humans, such as a monetary debt, the claims of God, such as the obligatory rituals and certain criminal penalties, are not subject to waiver *(isqât)*, but they may be subject to special excuses: for example, menstruating women are exempted from prayer by a dispensation *(rukhsa)*. There is disagreement whether stratagems *(hiyal,* sing. *hîla)* may be employed to escape claims of either sort.

A third classification serves to organize the subject matter of the substantive law under such headings as ritual law *('ibâdât)*, family law *(munâkahât,* "matrimonial matters"), commercial law *(mu'âmalât)*, and criminal law *('uqûbât,* "punishments"). The ritual law is distinguished from the other areas of the law in the extent to which it rests on detailed provisions of the Qur'an and Sunna to the exclusion of analogy, which by its nature is inapplicable to matters resisting rational analysis.

The scope of classic Islamic law is extremely broad, ranging from details of ablutions required for prayer to the structure of the Islamic state (see "Islamic Government," chapter 11). Not all areas of law, however, were equally developed. Greatest attention was devoted to the elaboration of the private law, including the ritual law, in its most minute details. By contrast, Islamic public law *(al-ahkâm al-sultâniyya)* was little cultivated, perhaps because the jurists had a very limited influence in shaping the institutions of the state, which early on fell into the hands of temporal rulers who could often be tyrants. Public-law doctrines tend to present an idealized account of the caliphate and other governmental offices, and only belatedly and grudgingly did many jurists come to acknowledge how far the reality had departed from the ideal.

There are several common misapprehensions about substantive law. Islamic law, at least as far as the doctrine is concerned, accords women property rights far more extensive than did Western law until quite recently. Even married women, for example, retain full control over the property they bring into the marriage (see "Women and Islam," chapter 12). In contrast, women are disadvantaged vis-à-vis men in the share of the estate they receive as heirs and are restricted from engaging fully in public life. The situation of non-Muslims, following other revealed faiths, such as Judaism and Christianity, is broadly comparable (see "Islam and Judaism," chapter 13, and "Islam and Christianity," chapter 14). As subjects of the Islamic state, they fall under its protection *(dhimma)* and are granted extensive rights to practice their religion and live their lives in accordance with its teachings, even to the point of retaining their own religious courts. Yet, like women, they are barred from filling various state offices and participating fully in public life. Islamic criminal law has a reputation for cruelty, no doubt stemming from such harsh prescribed punishments as stoning for certain cases of fornication, and amputation for theft, both among the crimes with defined penalties *(hudûd,* sing. *hadd).* In the absence of a confession, however, the standard of proof for these so-called *hudûd* crimes is high: four upstanding male eyewitnesses in the case of fornication, two in the case of theft. What is more, the jurists developed numerous substantive exculpatory doctrines that tended greatly to minimize the application of corporal and capital punishment.

Islamic Law in Practice

As a religious law, Islamic law binds individual Muslims, including the ruler and other governmental officials, and threatens those who violate its prescriptions with punishment in the hereafter. Islamic law itself also provides for the exercise of coercion in this world, above all in the resolution of disputes. The power that can apply such coercion flows, according to juristic theory, from the single figure at the head of the state, ideally an elected caliph, but in practice far more often a self-imposed temporal ruler *(sultân).* In keeping with this theory, the authority of the *qâdî* (judge) and other state officials has its source in a delegation from the ruler. Islamic law recognizes the authority of the ruler to supplement the law of the jurists with such administrative measures as are necessary for the welfare of his subjects and are not in conflict with the clear prescriptions of the revealed texts *(siyâsa shar'iyya,* "administration within the scope of the Shari'a"). But state regulations did not always remain within the boundaries of the Shari'a, and complaints about crimes and punishments not sanctioned by Islam, and un-Islamic taxes, are common.

Given the geographic and temporal scope of Islamic civilization, the question of how fully Islamic law was actually implemented at any given time and place cannot be given a simple answer. The traditional *qâdî's* court *(mahkama)* has jurisdiction over cases of all kinds, and since such courts were a regular feature of premodern Muslim societies, we may assume that Islamic law enjoyed a considerable measure of respect. The recurrent appearance throughout Islamic history of revivalist movements and regimes testifies to a continuing concern for the full implementation of the Shari'a. Any further generalizations would be hazardous. It is safe to say that there was widespread compliance with the ritual law (except for the alms-tax on wealth) and with family law, although Islamic law was sometimes in competition with local customary law in such matters as inheritance.

The Shari'a in Modern Times

The ascendancy of the Western powers vis-à-vis the leading Muslim states, increasingly evident in the nineteenth century, led to a marked diminution in the role of the Shari'a in Muslim societies. In some cases the authority of the Shari'a was curtailed directly by colonial powers, such as the British in India or the French in Algeria, who introduced radical changes in the legal systems over which they assumed control. In other cases, Muslim governments set about reforming their judicial systems along Western lines. In both cases, the formerly general jurisdiction of the Shari'a courts shrank and, along with it, the standing of the traditionally trained *qâdîs*. Characteristic of these developments are the appearance of law codes modeled after those of Europe, even when the content was Islamic, as in the Ottoman Civil Code *(Mecelle)* of 1877, and the rise of new legal personnel, including judges and lawyers whose legal education no longer emphasized mastery of the jurisprudential texts.

Among those devoted to Islamic law, one response to the crisis of Western domination was a call for a renewal of Islamic law to render it suitable for the novel circumstances into which Muslims had been thrust. The reformers, led by the Egyptian Muhammad 'Abduh (d. 1905) and his Syrian disciple Muhammad Rashîd Ridâ (d. 1935), regarded the aura of sanctity that had come to surround the law of the legal schools as a major obstacle to their goals. Drawing upon a distinguished line of premodern critics of *taqlîd* — the unquestioning acceptance of earlier rulings — whose writings they were instrumental in disseminating, they called for a

49

revival of *ijtihâd*. The modern reformers had in mind a radical revision of the classical law. This revision they undertook in part by championing long-abandoned minority opinions preserved in the vast legal *(fiqh)* literature and by elevating to prominence doctrines that had hitherto been relegated to marginal status in legal theory. Thus they made frequent appeal to the welfare *(maslaha)* of the Muslims as the basis for doing away with old institutions and establishing new ones, as well as to "dire necessity" *(darûra)* as grounds for temporarily suspending the application of prohibitions such as the one against usury *(ribâ)*.

The upshot of these developments was that with few exceptions the many Muslim nation-states that emerged in the twentieth century had legal systems that limited the sphere of the application of the Shari'a to family law, often in the form of a code incorporating restrictions on polygamy and the unilateral repudiation of wives *(talâq)*, justified as instances of the modern *ijtihâd* called for by the reformers. While this situation may have had the support of the ruling Westernized elites, it was profoundly unsatisfactory to Shari'a scholars, traditional and reformist, and to the common people. Calls for a return to a full implementation of Islamic law became increasingly widespread in the 1970s, and in response to such pressures constitutions were in some cases amended to provide for the Shari'a (or the principles of the Shari'a) as a principal source of national legislation (e.g., Syria in 1973).

Concurrently, the reformist agenda of undermining the authority of the traditional schools of legal thought proved to be extraordinarily successful, particularly in the Arab Middle East, where it often went hand in hand with the adoption of a *salafî* (literally "early [Muslim]," i.e., fundamentalist or literalist) theology. Very few traditional jurists have been able to escape contact with reformist thought, and reformist and more traditional jurists now commonly collaborate in the various international academies for the study of Islamic law, such as those attached to the Muslim World League (1978) and the Organization of the Islamic Conference (1981). These academies are engaged in addressing a host of modern problems, including those stemming from recent efforts to create banks and other financial institutions that operate in accordance with Islamic law. In addition, individual reformist jurists have been able to achieve considerable influence, and their legal opinions are widely disseminated in print and through radio, television, videos, and the Internet. Those participating in this revival of legal thought commonly regard their work as marking an indispensable preparatory stage toward the integral application of the Shari'a.

Steps toward a fuller implementation of the Shari'a, often by the introduction of Islamic criminal law, have already been taken in a number of places (e.g., Afghanistan, Pakistan, Sudan, and northern Nigeria), most dramatically and successfully in the Islamic Republic of Iran. The return to the Shari'a, however, has not generally led to the abolition of such borrowed institutions as constitutions, codes of law, and the bar, which far from being regarded as alien to the Shari'a, are now seen as essential to its successful reintroduction. The worldwide resurgence of Islam and the efforts to implement the Shari'a, often vaguely defined, raise justified concerns among Muslims and non-Muslims that, unless drastically reinterpreted, Islamic law will adversely affect the rights of such classes as women, homosexuals, other Muslim minorities, and non-Muslims. The efforts by progressive Muslims (e.g., Tariq Ramadan) to reformulate Islamic law in such sensitive areas have so far failed to gain wide popular support.

Chapter Six

ISLAMIC PHILOSOPHY

Jon McGinnis

Dialectical Theology *(Kalâm)*

Muslim thinkers' first taste of philosophical speculation seems to have been through dialectical theology *(kalâm)*, which drew on indigenous sources for inspiration, namely, the Arabic language, the Qur'an, the Hadith, and Islamic jurisprudence *(fiqh)*. Historically there were three principal schools of *kalâm:* the rationalist Mu'tazilî school of thought (from *i'tizâl*, "to stand apart"), the more traditionally inclined Ash'arî school of thought (named for al-Ash'arî [d. 935]), and the Mâturîdî school of thought (named for al-Mâturîdî [d. 944]) falling between the two. The Mu'tazilîs frequently rejected literal readings of the Qur'an, maintaining that it had to be interpreted through the lens of what reason demands. For example, while the Qur'an ascribes a number of attributes to God, such as sight, hearing, power, and will, the Mu'tazilîs argued that these, taken at face value, undermine divine unity *(tawhîd)*, because if there are distinct attributes in God and each one of them is divine, then there would be multiple divine things, all equally deserving of being a divinity, which contradicts the Muslim creed: "There is no god but God." For the same reason, the Mu'tazilîs argued that the Qur'an could not literally be the uncreated word of God, but had to be created; if it were not, then it too would have to be eternal and worthy of being a divinity. Mu'tazilîs also denied the doctrine of divine determinism, which reserved all causal efficacy for God, arguing that if God were to determine every act, including human acts of volition — such as to sin or to submit to God — then divine justice would be jeopardized.

Mu'tazilism, however, never had broad theological appeal. Thus, in response to the Mu'tazilîs' (overly) rationalistic interpretation of Islam, al-Ash'arî (and al-Mâturîdî) offered a more moderate philosophical theology, one that came to dominate theological speculation, at least in Sunni Islam (see "Sunnis, Sunnism," chapter 9). Unlike most traditionalists, who distrusted the application of reason and logic to the Qur'an, al-Ash'arî had been trained as a Mu'tazilî and appreciated the value of reason, particularly in refuting the deficiencies he found in Mu'tazilî thought. However, al-Ash'arî also thought the application of reason had limits, which, he argued, were reached when it came to things divine: one simply had to rely on what the Qur'an said about God. Thus, al-Ash'arî affirmed God's attributes and the Qur'an's uncreatedness. Also, for al-Ash'arî, while God does will and create every event on Earth, humans nonetheless acquire *(kasb)* responsibility for those actions, good or bad. These doctrines, al-Ash'arî maintained, have to be accepted without asking how *(bi-lâ kayf)*.

When it came to the created order, Mu'tazilîs and Ash'arîs were more generally in agreement. They both argued that the world was created in the finite past. For if the world had existed infinitely into the past, then an infinite number of days must have been traversed in order to reach the present day, and it was agreed by virtually everyone that it is impossible completely to traverse an infinite. Therefore, one must be able to go back to some first moment when the world was created and before which it did not exist. This argument provided the basis for the *kalâm* proof for the existence of God, for there cannot be something that is created unless there is a Creator.

God's Existence

Falsafa was the Arabic rendering of Greek *philosophia,* and its practitioners saw themselves as the immediate heirs and continuators of the Greek philosophical-scientific worldview of Plato, Aristotle, and the Neoplatonic commentators. Historically the most important question treated in *falsafa* was about the existence of God. While no Muslim philosopher denied God's existence, virtually all felt compelled to provide proof for it, in particular to show that there is only one God and that God is absolutely simple, that is, that there is no composition within the deity. This theme was itself continued well beyond the classical period and still very much dominated the postclassical scene. The most common *falsafa* argument for divine simplicity noted that if there were composition in God, there must be some cause uniting the disparate parts so that there is one God — for a thing was thought to exist insofar as it functions as a unified whole — and yet if anything were the cause of God's unity, that cause would in fact be God.

In the classical period the most common strategy to prove God's existence began with an analysis of existence itself *(aysa, huwiyya, wujûd)*, dividing it into two distinct kinds of existents, one causally dependent upon the other. It continued by showing that the nondependent existent is so precisely because of its simplicity. Al-Kindî (d. ca. 866), the "First Arabic Philosopher," for example, divided existence into that which is unified and that which involves multiplicity, where that existence that has multiplicity within it requires what is absolutely unified to bring about an association of the multiple parts. Al-Fârâbî (d. ca. 950) presented a "perfect being ontology," which distinguished between what is absolutely perfect and that which, while imperfect in some respect, has different grades of perfection, where "perfection" *(tâmm* or *kamâl)* is understood as that which completes a thing in its being. At the high end of this chain there must be that which lacks nothing in order to complete its being, and which completes the being of everything else. Were this completely perfect being not absolutely one, it would not be absolutely perfect, needing a cause to unify it.

Ibn-Sîna (Avicenna, d. 1037) conceptually divided existents into that which exists necessarily of itself and that which exists possibly of itself. The former, should it exist, would be that which is not dependent or conditioned upon anything else for its existence. Now if it were composed of parts, then, since wholes depend upon their parts, the whole of it would be dependent upon another, namely, upon its part (since parts are other than the whole). Consequently, what is necessary through itself would not be necessary through itself — an obvious contradiction. Thus, what is necessary of itself must be absolutely one and simple. What exists only possibly in itself, on the other hand, is that which in some way is dependent or conditioned upon another, and so caused. Ibn-Sîna then considered the set of all things possible in themselves, and observed that that set cannot be necessary since it is composed of parts, and so the set must be something possible in itself. Inasmuch as it is possible in itself, it is dependent upon another. That other could be one of the members of the set of all and only things possible in themselves, or something outside of the set. If the set is dependent upon one of its members, then, since that member is the cause of the existence of every member within the set, it exists through itself and so would not be dependent upon another. In that case, the member would exist necessarily of itself, but only things existing possibly of themselves were included within the set. Thus there is a contradiction. Therefore, concluded Ibn-Sîna, the set of all things possible in themselves must depend upon something that exists outside the set of possible things, and the only thing outside the set of all things possible in themselves is something that exists necessarily of itself, namely, God.

Cosmos

The most disputed cosmological question within the classical and postclassical periods involved the creation of the cosmos and its dependence upon God. The question was not whether God created the cosmos, but whether God has from all eternity been creating it *(ibdâ')* or whether he created it at some moment in the finite past *(hudûth)*. Most philosophers maintained that the world is eternal: a preferred argument derived from the nature of the deity. So, for example, both al-Fârâbî and Ibn-Sîna maintained that if God went from not creating to creating, that would entail a change in God, but if God changes in any way, then there must be some cause of that change. In that case, there would be some cause acting upon the Cause of all causes, and so God would fail to be perfect, necessary, and so on. More specifically, they argued that God must create either essentially or accidentally. Now, were anything to belong to God accidentally, there would be composition within God; however, there are good philosophical reasons for affirming the absolute simplicity of God. Consequently, should God create, He must do so essentially, but since God's essence has existed eternally, they concluded that what flows or emanates *(faydân)* from that essence, namely, the created order, must also be eternal.

Still, some thinkers argued that one could demonstrate the temporal createdness of the cosmos. In addition to al-Kindî, who provided his own version of the *kalâm* argument from the impossibility of traversing an infinite, al-Ghazâlî (d. 1111) argued that since virtually all the philosophers also maintained that the human soul is immortal, that is, it continues to exist forever after the death of the body, if the world existed infinitely into the past, then right now there should presently exist an actual infinity of immortal human souls, which most thinkers within even the *falsafa* tradition would have denied.

Two novel approaches to the issue of the world's eternity appeared in Islamic Spain. Ibn-Tufayl (d. ca. 1185) held that the world's age could not be determined, but it did not matter, since whether the world was created from nothing at some time in the finite past or has been eternally created, it follows that there is an infinitely powerful Creator, God. Ibn-Rushd (Averroës, d. 1198) argued that the controversy over the world's age came down to semantics. Time, he maintained, is cyclical. Thus in a very real sense time is finite, in the way a circle is, so an infinite is never traversed, but since it is cyclical it can go on without ceasing — and so God never undergoes a change from not creating to creating, for he is the eternal cause of the cosmos's perpetual motion.

A unique approach to the question of the creation of the cosmos was the Persian Mullâ Sadrâ's (d. 1640) doctrine of substantial motion *(haraka jismiyya)*, which maintains that in order for a substance to undergo any accidental change, such as a change of place, quantity, quality, or even position, there must be a change in the subject underlying those accidents, namely, the substance itself. Since accidental changes are continuously occurring in the cosmos, the very substance of the created world must be continuously changing such that new substances are continuously coming to be from what previously was nonexistent. Using this theory, Mullâ Sadrâ saw a way to reconcile the occasionalism of *kalâm* with the emanation theories of *falsafa*, for God must re-create the cosmos at every moment from nothing, as *kalâm* would have it, but he does so through a continuous, uninterrupted emanation, as *falsafa* would have it.

The Human Soul

All thinkers within the *falsafa* tradition maintained that the human soul is (in some sense) immortal, even if they denied a bodily resurrection. That souls exist was taken to be self-evident, for the soul is whatever explains why a living thing performs the functions or activities that typify it as living. Thus, inasmuch as living things are different from nonliving things, the living things must have something that the nonliving things do not, namely, what explains those unique life-activities. That thing, whatever it is, is simply called "soul" *(nafs)*, that is, a principle of animation. As for showing that the soul is immortal, their general strategy was to argue that the soul or some aspect of it is immaterial and that only what is associated with matter can undergo corruption so as to cease to exist. Corruption involves the loss of a species-form — that is, that form that makes some material to be the kind of thing it is — and that form's being replaced by a new species-form. Hence, for something to undergo corruption it must be a composite of both form and matter. Their argument for the soul's immateriality began by considering the human function of understanding or grasping universal concepts, such as humanity, equinity, and so forth. They reasoned that since universal concepts are wholly intellectual and nonsensible, they must be immaterial, and only something that is itself immaterial could be effected by such immaterial concepts. So, for example, al-Fârâbi argued that while the human soul is initially the form of a body, and so requires matter, as one intellectually develops, a power within the soul must gradually separate from matter, eventually reaching a point when it is self-reflective and in fact immaterial. Ibn-Sîna, in contrast, was a dualist, arguing that from the moment one's soul comes to be, it is an immaterial substance that merely uses the body, a material substance, as its tool. Consequently, since the soul is not associated with matter in any respect, and only what is material is corruptible, it must be incorruptible, and so is immortal.

Mystical Concepts

While there is a debate concerning to what extent, if any, Ibn-Sîna was sympathetic to mystical speculation, there is no question that his thought provided the philosophical machinery for later Sufis to articulate their mystical experiences in philosophical terms and categories (see "Sufism," chapter 7). Ironically, however, perhaps the one most responsible for reinterpreting Ibn-Sîna along Sufi lines was the arch-critic of the *falsafa* movement itself, al-Ghazâlî. While al-Ghazâlî leveled a devastating attack of *falsafa* in his *Incoherence of the Philosophers,* he also appropriated many of Ibn-Sîna's philosophical concepts — albeit recasting them in Qur'anic language — in order to provide a more rigorous presentation of *kalâm,* while at the same time introducing Sufi elements into *kalâm.* With these first steps toward amalgamating *kalâm, falsafa,* and Sufi mysticism, al-Ghazâlî might be thought of as ushering in the postclassical period of Islamic philosophy.

This same synthesizing tendency can also be seen in the illuminationist philosophy of al-Suhrawardî (d. 1191), particularly in his proof for the existence and unity of God, where one sees a more figurative albeit equally rigorous analysis of existence as his classical predecessors but one that now employs light imagery as well as Qur'anic and mystical language. Al-Suhrawardî divided existence into that which is essentially light or luminous and that which does not have light of itself, and so is of itself dark or dusky, even though it may receive an accidental light from what has light essentially. He argued that since there cannot be an infinite causal chain, the series of lights must terminate at a Light of lights. This Light of lights, which he argues must be an incorporeal light, has to be one and simple; for incorporeal lights cannot differ in their true nature as incorporeal light. Thus if there were either more than one Light of lights or distinct parts within the Light of lights, something must be causally acting upon it to bring about the difference. Yet, the Light of lights is the Cause of causes, and so is not causally acted upon but is that which only acts.

Not all mystics were so ready to embrace *falsafa*. Thus, the rationalizing mystic Ibn-ʿArabî (d. 1240) railed against the philosophers' analysis of existence to prove that there is a wholly simple God. The philosophers' approach, argues Ibn-ʿArabî, loses sight of the underlying unity of all things, the unity of Being itself *(wahdat al-wujûd)*. Only through mystical practice can one come to know God, wherein one can become one with God to the extent that that is possible, at which point Being becomes absolutely transparent to the knower.

The seemingly incompatible doctrines of Ibn-Sîna (and his analysis of existence, with its emphasis on necessary and possible existents) and Ibn-ʿArabî (and his insistence on the unity of Being) are brought together in the mystical philosopher Mullâ Sadrâ and his doctrine of the gradation or modulation of Being or Existence *(tashkîk al-wujûd)*. While all of existence is one, for him there are degrees of intensity of being, just as light is one inasmuch as it is light, and yet lights can vary in intensity. Thus God is Existence or Being *(wujûd)* without any admixture of privation such that there could be some other existence that He does not possess, whereas everything else lacks some existence of itself, and as one falls further and further away from Existence or Being a hierarchy of being is formed. Just as the beams from the sun are not identical with the sun, neither are they something wholly distinct from the sun. Here one sees Ibn-Sîna's analysis of necessary and possible existence, al-Suhrawardî's light imagery, and Ibn-ʿArabi's insistence on the unity of Being, all come together. Mullâ Sadrâ's magnum opus is *The Four Journeys,* a grand synthesis of of *falsafa, kalâm,* Sufism, and Islam itself.

Modern Concerns

Many of the major philosophical themes of the classical and postclassical periods involved what is beyond the here and now, namely, a focus on God and the afterlife, and turning in on one's self until the self is annihilated in a mystical experience of God. In contrast, the modern period might best be typified as turning outward and developing the self so as to become a conduit for divine grace through political activity and social justice. The founder of Islamic modernism is usually identified as Shâh Walî Allâh (d. 1762), who lived in Mughal India at the time of its decline. He attributed the loss of Muslim power and influence to the divisiveness he saw in fellow Muslims — whether between schools of Islamic legal thought, Sunnis and Shi'ites, or mystics and theologians — as well as the lack of Islamic values among leaders and followers alike. To remedy this, he advocated a theory of conciliation *(tatbîq)*, which emphasized the common and shared principles on which the diverse opinions of his time rested. To justify his theory of conciliation, he drew upon one of the principal doctrines of the postclassical period, the unity of Existence or Being *(wahdat al-wujûd)*, and developed a theory of the unity of testaments or experiences *(wahdat al-shuhûd)*. The general idea is that since the principle of all things, God, is absolutely unified, the experiences and descriptions of the world and God by the various Muslim opinions must in principle be reconcilable. His hope was that once he had explained and mediated the various divisive tendencies, a true *ijtihâd*, exerting or striving, for social and religious development and reform would be realized.

Following in the footsteps of Shâh Walî Allâh is the philosopher-poet Muhammad Iqbâl (d. 1938). While he did not have a philosophical system as such, Iqbâl did present substantive philosophical material in his books, poetry, and lectures, stressing the development of the self as opposed to mystical annihilation. In fact, he viewed certain forms of mysticism, namely, those that view Being or God as static rather than dynamic, and focus inward rather than outward, as one of the primary causes of Islam's decline and loss of vitality in the modern world. In the same vein, Iqbâl urged that Platonic ontology, which so informed earlier Islamic philosophy, with its emphasis on the impassive nature of Being or Existence, be replaced with a process ontology, like Henri Bergson's with its emphasis on vitality and creative evolution. Iqbâl also advocated for a union of religion and science that uses technology to improve one's material conditions here and now.

Revitalizing, rethinking, and making Islam relevant to the contemporary world have remained a central theme among contemporary Muslim philosophers, such as the Iranian philosopher of religion Abdolkarim Soroush (b. 1945) and the Algerian Mohammad Arkoun (d. 2010). Fundamental to Soroush's work is distinguishing between religion as divinely revealed and the sociohistorical understanding of religion. Central to Arkoun's work is the role that Muslim philosophers have historically played in the development and articulation of the philosophy that grew up around the Mediterranean, and thus the shared ties between the Islamic and European intellectual traditions. Like Shâh Walî Allâh centuries before him, Arkoun points to monotheism, a common principle shared among Jews, Christians, and Muslims that can be used as a basis for reconciling the apparently dissonant claims of these religions. Again like Shâh Walî Allâh, Arkoun and others have called for a renewed *ijtihâd,* now understood as a (re)interpretation of Islam, and like for Iqbâl before him, such an *ijtihâd* must involve the union of Islam and modern methodologies such as developments in hermeneutical theory, literary criticism, history, and all that the social scientists have to offer.

Chapter Seven

SUFISM

Ahmet T. Karamustafa

Term

"Sufism" is an Anglicism widely used to describe the beliefs and practices of Sufis. Sufi (Arabic *sûfî*, probably from *sûf*, "wool") originally designated individuals (who perhaps wore woolen garments), specifically ascetics who believed in renunciation of this world. From the middle of the ninth century, however, *sûfî* came to be used increasingly as a technical term to designate a group of people who belonged to a clearly identifiable social movement in Iraq, especially Baghdad, based on a distinct type of mystical piety. The most prominent members of this movement were Abû-Sa'îd al-Kharrâz (d. ca. 899), Abû-al-Husayn al-Nûrî (d. 907), and Junayd al-Baghdâdî (d. 910). In time, the Baghdad mystics began to use the name Sufi for themselves; the word then no longer signified "wool-wearing renunciant" but came to be applied to the mystics of Baghdad. This new, distinctive form of pious living was in turn dubbed *tasawwuf*, "living as a Sufi."

Early Muslim Mystics

While Sufism was taking shape in Baghdad, individuals and social groups with similar views and practices were to be found among Muslim communities in other locations, even though the latter were not initially known as Sufis. Most notable among these were Sahl al-Tustarî (d. ca. 896) in Iraq, al-Hakîm al-Tirmidhî (d. 910) in central Asia, and a group of mystics in northeastern Iran known as the "People of Blame" (the Malâmatiyya). These mystics differed from Baghdad Sufis and from each other in thought and practice, but they gradually blended with the mystics of Baghdad, and in time they too came to be identified as Sufis. The origins of these distinct Muslim mystic groups are obscure, and the possible influence of earlier religious traditions, most notably Christian asceticism, on the emergence of Islamic mysticism remains unresolved.

The early Muslim mystics were most concerned with obtaining experiential knowledge *(ma'rifa)* of God's unity. In the Sufi perspective, human beings, viewed as God-servants, had experienced proximity to their Lord before the beginning of time, when all human beings, in spirit, stood witness to God's lordship on the Day of the Covenant (Q 7:172), and they were promised an even more intimate closeness to him at the end of time in Paradise. While on Earth, however, they had to strive to preserve and renew the memory of their primordial proximity to their Creator by turning their backs on everything other than God and by living their lives in constant recognition of his presence. In practice, this orientation meant training and domestication of the lower self through continuous cultivation of the heart. The latter was understood as the spiritual organ of God's presence in the human person, and its chief sustenance was remembrance or mention of God through "invocation" *(dhikr)* and "hearing/witnessing God" *(samâ', a term that later came to be associated with poetry and music).

The Sufi Path to Friendship with God

Paradoxically, the journey *(sulûk)* toward the Lord started only when the Sufi realized his or her own weakness as an agent and acknowledged God as the only true actor in the universe. This journey was normally envisaged as a path *(tarîq* or *tarîqa)* marked by various stations *(maqâm)* and states *(hâl)*. Closeness to God was thought to entail a sharp turn from the concerns of this lower world *(dunyâ)* toward the realm of ultimate matters *(âkhira)*, a movement away from the lower self *(nafs)* toward the inner locus of God's presence *(qalb,* literally "heart"), but it proved difficult to characterize the final encounter with God located at the end of the journey. While some, like al-Kharrâz and al-Nûrî, described the highest stage of intimacy with God as the dissolution of all self-consciousness, others like Junayd viewed the ultimate goal as a "reconstituted" self, a human identity recomposed in the image of God after being thoroughly deconstructed during the Sufi journey. All agreed, however, that the ultimate Sufi experience was to be viewed as the passing away or reabsorption of the created human being into the only true/real *(Haqq)* being of God and, most emphatically, not as a divinization of the human. The Sufi could, so to speak, flow into God, but movement in the other direction was off-limits, or at the very least extremely limited, since such a flow from the divine into the human could pave the way to divinization of the human and thus lead to the suspect, even heretical, doctrines of incarnation and divine inherence *(hulûl)*.

Whatever their approach to the thorny issue of encounter with the divine, those who shared the common aim of drawing close to God through experiential knowing enjoyed a special camaraderie with one another in the form of circles of fellowship, mutual mentoring, and relationships of master and disciple. Not all human beings became wayfarers, or grew close to God: that privilege was reserved for the few "friends" or "intimates" of God *(walî,* pl. *awliyâ'),* who were highly conscious of their special status and came to be seen as the spiritual elect. Many "friends," much like the prophets, saw themselves as God's special agents among humans, rendered distinct by their special status as intermediaries between the divine and the human planes of being. According to this view, they channeled God's mercy to humankind and served to increase God-consciousness among the otherwise heedless and self-absorbed human race through their personal example and their tireless advocacy of God's cause in human affairs.

The special status of the friends manifested itself in a number of practices that simultaneously underscored their distinctness from common believers and served to forge bonds of fellowship, loyalty, and mutual allegiance among the spiritual elect. They assembled in certain places of congregation and traveled in groups, developed distinctive prayer rituals in the form of the invocation and listening to poetry and music that frequently led to rapture or ecstasy *(wajd),* and adopted special initiation practices, notably investiture with a woolen robe *(khirqa).*

Spread and Growth

During the course of the tenth century, Sufism spread to regions beyond Iraq and blended with indigenous mystical trends elsewhere. Its diffusion throughout Muslim communities went apace with the emergence of a normative Sufi tradition, as evidenced clearly in the appearance of a specialized literature that was self-consciously about Sufis and Sufism. The normativization of Sufism corresponds exactly with the normativizaton of theology and law: Sufism is one of the classical expressions of Islam as it takes shape as an international religion.

Two major genres grew out of historical reports about individual Sufis: the survey and the biographical compilation. These two genres were sometimes combined in the form of discrete sections in a single work, and the material they conveyed was compiled and packaged in various ways to serve different but related functions: pedagogical guidance of those who aspired to become Sufis, pious commemoration of past masters, the building of corporate solidarity among Sufis, and confident self-presentation and self-assertion vis-à-vis other groups competing for authority within Muslim communities.

The specialized Sufi literature of the tenth and eleventh centuries was produced by Sufis of two divergent orientations: the "traditionalists," who were averse to all scholarship that assigned a prominent role to human reason, and the "academic" Sufis, who, in contrast, were aligned with legal and theological scholarship. The latter approach, popularized by al-Ghazâlî (d. 1111) in his seminal work, *Reviving the Religious Sciences,* gradually but surely assumed authoritative status throughout all Muslim communities, especially among educated elites.

Spiritual Lineages and Orders

The shaping of Sufism as a distinct tradition was evident also in the "spiritual lineages" *(silsila)* that developed around major Sufi masters *(shaykh),* who placed a special emphasis on training disciples *(murîd).* Such spiritually linked communities took some time to develop, and the different stages of this development are difficult to document. Increasingly, aspirants who were accepted as novices by a *shaykh* were not only initiated into Sufism but also inducted into a particular lineage held together by bonds of loyalty and devotion extending from the novices and experienced disciples to the master, and by bonds of guidance and protection extending in the other direction. The aspirants submitted to the authority of the master with complete trust; in return, the master pledged to guide them to their goal and to protect them from dangers on the path of spiritual development. This "guide-novice" relationship (often known as *suhba*) was increasingly solemnized through initiation and graduation ceremonies that involved elements such as an oath of allegiance *(bay'a)* and a handclasp during the initial instruction of the invocation formula *(dhikr)*, as well as the bestowal of a "certificate of graduation" *(ijâza)* accompanied by special insignia, most notably a cloak *(khirqa)*, when the novices attained their goal.

The rise to prominence of the guide-novice relationship led to the gradual formation of spiritual lineages, some of which were powerful enough to spawn actual social communities held together through devotion to a particular master. Perhaps the most visible social manifestation of these new spiritual families and the main social locus for the formation of communities around them was the growing social visibility of the residential Sufi lodge *(ribât, khânqah)*, which by the end of the eleventh century grew into a durable social institution from its tentative beginnings a century or more earlier. With the establishment of lodges as prominent social institutions, Sufi spiritual lineages were slowly but surely being woven into the fabric of the greater society around them.

Remarkably, the ascendancy of masters who increasingly came to preside over communities of Sufis residing in lodges coincided with the rise to prominence among Muslims of cults of saints. Originally based on belief in the existence of a divinely appointed company of saints, cults of saints began to take shape already during the ninth and tenth centuries, and were doubtless in full bloom by the eleventh century, when clear reflections of this popular practice began to appear in intellectual life. In practical terms, the saint cults manifested themselves as an ideological and ritual complex organized around the basic concept of spiritual power or blessing *(baraka)* and the ritualistic performance of visiting tombs and other holy places *(ziyâra)*. Even though Sufis by no means had a monopoly on popular sainthood in this period, they easily constituted the majority of the saints.

Through this conjunction of the Sufi and the popular spheres of sainthood, Sufism gradually ceased to be a form of piety that appealed almost exclusively to the urban middle and upper-middle classes and began to spread through the whole social canvas of premodern Islamic societies, from political elites to wage earners in urban centers to peasants and nomads in the countryside. Sainthood increasingly came to be defined almost exclusively in Sufi terms, and Sufi masters began to exercise considerable power in all spheres of social life.

From the twelfth century onward, when Sufism became mainstream, the Sufi presence in Islamic societies took the form of distinct social groupings generally known as orders *(tarîqa*, pl. *turuq)*. These were concrete, institutional mappings of spiritual lineages onto the social fabric in the form of networks of lodges. Often built and maintained as pious endowments *(awqâf,* sing. *waqf),* these lodges frequently doubled as tomb-shrines that evolved into centers for saint cults. Since the twelfth century, orders of local, regional, and international scope have proliferated in all Muslim communities. The most widespread and durable among these have been the Qâdirî, Naqshbandî, Shâdhilî, and Khalwatî orders, followed by such regional orders as the Chishtî (India) and the Mevlevi (Turkey). The orders represent an extremely wide range of Sufi activity at different levels of institutionalization, and they continue even now to define Sufism among Muslims.

Expansion of Influence

The twelfth century was also a watershed for the spiritual, intellectual, and artistic landscape of Sufism. Up until that point, Sufis had largely maintained an inward orientation. However, the alignment of this distinct form of piety with legal and theological scholarship opened the floodgates through which legal, theological, and philosophical thinking could flow into Sufism. Indeed, from the end of the eleventh century, Sufis began to open up to all the different intellectual discourses that were available in Islamic societies, and not only legal, theological, and philosophical speculation but also the whole array of "occult sciences" — including interpretation of dreams and other visionary experiences, as well as divination and prognostication — gradually found its way into Sufi thought. At the same time, Sufism blended with other forms of piety such as messianism, apocalypticism, and esoterism.

The expansion of the scope of Sufi thought and practice to all levels and aspects of social and intellectual life in this period also resulted in an unprecedented literary and artistic fluorescence. Cultivation of poetic and musical expression, which had been a special feature of Sufism from its very beginnings, now reached new artistic heights in all the different linguistic and musical traditions prevalent in Muslim communities. This confluence of Sufism with all other major intellectual, artistic, and spiritual trends conspired to produce a stellar array of seminal Sufi figures during this period, of whom Abû-Madyan (d. 1197), Najm-al-dîn Kubrâ (d. 1221), Ibn-ʿArabî (d. 1240), and Jâlal-al-dîn Rûmî (d. 1273) are prominent examples.

The almost complete blending of Sufism into all forms of social and cultural life from the twelfth century onward makes it practically impossible to write the subsequent history of Sufism as a self-contained tradition of mystical thought and practice, since in a very real sense all subsequent Islamic history was at least colored if not permeated by Sufi themes and practices. This was, at least in part, a result of Sufism's flexibility in accommodating and tolerating practices and beliefs emanating from the other religious and philosophical systems Islam encountered. In the following centuries, Sufism spread west to Egypt, North Africa, Spain, and West Africa, and east to India, central Asia, China, and Southeast Asia. In some instances there was a close relationship between the ruling dynasty and Sufism, such as in Seljuk and Ghaznavid patronage of Sufi institutions, and Indian and Acehnese patronage of Sufi scholarship. The origins of the Safavid dynasty, which ruled Iran from 1502 to 1736, were in a Sufi order; and in twentieth-century Senegal, the Mouride brotherhood (in Arabic, Murîdiyya), a branch of the Qâdiriyya, has come to exercise enormous political power nationally.

Sufism continues to be a vibrant mode of piety in Muslim communities throughout the globe. Although Sufi thought and practices have come under heavy and sustained criticism from many rationalizing Muslim modernists who view mystical piety as antithetical to "development and progress," and from many conservative and neoconservative movements who view Sufism as avowedly heterodox, Sufi orientations remain attractive to a broad array of Muslims who cherish this spiritually and artistically rich aspect of their religious tradition. Traditional Sufi orders are active in practically all Muslim-majority settings, and new orders continue to appear with some frequency. Sufism has also established a lasting foothold in the West, as the establishment of orders in Europe and North America attests. Clearly, the Sufis have succeeded in conveying the significance and urgency of their central concern, which was to obtain experiential knowledge *(ma'rifa)* of God's unity by distilling the reality of the Islamic profession of faith, "There is no god but God," into their daily lives, and doing so for the great majority of their fellow Muslims from all walks of life.

Chapter Eight

SHI'ITES, SHI'ISM

Abdulaziz Sachedina

Term

The word "Shi'ism" is an Anglicization based on the Arabic term *Shî'ah*, "a separate or distinct party of people who follow or conform with one another," which is itself an abbreviation of *Shî'at 'Alî*, "the party of 'Alî." Broadly speaking, Shi'ites *(shî'î)* are Muslims who hold that the family (*ahl al-bayt*, literally "people of the house") of the Prophet Muhammad (d. 632) has a privileged position in the political and religious leadership (*imâma*) of the Muslim community. When used in the specific sense of partisans, Shi'ites are all who believe that 'Alî-ibn-Abî-Tâlib (d. 661), cousin and son-in-law of Muhammad, was the legitimate head and spiritual leader *(imâm)* of the Muslim polity. They regard him as the ultimate authority on questions of law and doctrine in Islam, having inherited the Prophet's political and religious authority immediately following his death. 'Alî would become the fourth caliph (ruled 656-661), and Sunnis would come to regard him and his predecessors as the four "rightly guided" *(râshidûn)* caliphs (see "Sunnis, Sunnism," chapter 9). But the Shi'ite belief in 'Alî's leadership would lead them to refuse to acknowledge the first three caliphs later recognized by the majority Sunni community — namely, Abû-Bakr (ruled 632-634), 'Umar (ruled 634-644), and 'Uthmân (ruled 644-656) — whom they considered usurpers of the leadership that rightfully belonged to 'Alî and his descendants.

Origins

The historical origins of the Shi'ite movement are difficult to reconstruct with certainty because of the biased presentation of its beginnings by both Sunni and Shi'ite historians and because all the available sources were recorded long after the events they describe. Modern Western scholars (and Sunnis themselves, of course), depending solely on Sunni sources, have generally dismissed Shi'ism as a heterodoxy that deviated from the majority Sunni orthodoxy. Accordingly, Shi'ites appear as followers of a political claimant who, having failed to establish an ideal Muslim rule, was gradually transformed into a religious figurehead. An objective reading of these tendentious sources, in light of the Shi'ite accounts of their own history, provides a different estimation of the Shi'ite minority movement.

Muhammad's message, as embodied in the Qur'an, provided immense spiritual as well as sociopolitical impetus for the establishment of the ideal community of Islam. Muhammad himself was not only the founder of a new religion but also the custodian of a new social order. Consequently, the question of leadership was the crucial issue that divided Muslims into various factions in the years following his death. The early years of Islamic history were characterized by a steady string of military victories under the first three caliphs. But as this period reached its end and civil wars broke out under 'Uthmân, the third caliph, contention arose over the necessity of qualified leadership to assume the office of Imam. Indeed, the revolt against 'Uthmân, his subsequent assassination, and the First Civil War were pivotal in the rise of the earliest Shi'ite movements proper.

Most of these early discussions about leadership took political form, but eventually the debates addressed the religious connection between divine guidance and the creation of an Islamic world order. These debates also highlighted the inevitable interdependence of the religious and the political in Islam. The rise of some prominent descendants of 'Alî as messianic saviors *(mahdî)* and the sympathetic, even enthusiastic, following they attracted reveal the tension felt in the awareness that the Islamic ideal lacked actualization in the real world, as well as the belief that it was the divinely guided Mahdî who could and would establish an ideal, just society (see below). Such expectations put the legitimacy of the Sunni caliphate in question, and the conflict between the supporters of 'Alî's claims and their opponents assumed a religious-theological, not simply a political, dimension.

Shi'ite Ideology

From the early days of Islam, some Muslims regarded the legitimate head of state not merely in political but also in religious terms (see "Islamic Government," chapter 11). They maintained that Muhammad himself held authority in all realms — spiritual and temporal, moral and civil. His spiritual authority included the power to interpret the message in the Qur'an without corrupting the revelation. Islam, to continue its function of directing the faithful toward the creation of a just and equitable order, needed a leader who could perform the Prophet's comprehensive role authoritatively. The exaltation of the Prophet and his rightful successor gave rise to the concept of a messianic Imam, the Mahdî, emanating from among the descendants of the Prophet to create an ideal Islamic community (messianism). The thrust of the Shi'ite ideology was the concept of the *wilâya* (authority) of 'Alî, who was the first to assert that the family of the Prophet had a special entitlement to lead the community. In fact, acknowledgment of 'Alî's *wilâya* became the sole criterion among Shi'ites for judging true faith.

The Shi'ite concept of Imam — which identified the legitimate head of state as God's caliph *(khalîfa)*, or deputy, on earth — was bound to meet with much resistance, since it demanded the recognition of 'Alî and his descendants as the imams with real control of Muslim polity. Furthermore, it also was a challenge to the Umayyad rulers (661-750) and a rallying point for all who felt discriminated against or mistreated by the ruling house. Consequently, from its inception Shi'ism functioned as an opposition party, challenging the performance of the government.

Religious Ramifications of Shi'ite Opposition

Several protest movements arose under a wide range of leaders from among 'Alî's descendants who were able to arouse in their followers a genuine religious urge to achieve sociopolitical goals. Shi'ite attempts at direct political action, however, were met with brutal resistance from the ruling dynasty, and their efforts quickly met with failure. The resultant frustration produced further Shi'ite factions. The radical factions insisted on armed resistance to the oppressive rule of the caliphate. These were also labeled *ghulât* (zealots, literally "exaggerators") by mainstream Shi'ites because of the extravagant claims they made about their imams (such as ascribing to them divine characteristics — omniscience, divine infusion, and the like). The moderate factions, having experienced the futility of direct political action, were prepared to postpone indefinitely the establishment of true Islamic rule under their messianic leader, the Mahdî. More than any other factor, the murder of the third Shi'ite Imam, Husayn, the younger son of 'Alî and Fâtima, the Prophet's daughter, and his followers by Umayyad troops at Karbala, Iraq, in 680, followed in 739 by the failure of the revolt of Zayd, Husayn's grandson, marked the turn toward a quietist attitude by these factions, who previously had been willing to fight for what they believed.

Shi'ite efforts until the time of the Abbasid victory in 750 were still lacking a well-formulated doctrine of the imamate. At that time Imam Ja'far al-Sâdiq (d. 765), who had been largely responsible for the moderation and discipline of the radical elements, provided Shi'ism with a sectarian credo. In the political turmoil of the eighth century, the imams had the opportunity to propagate Shi'ite viewpoints without inhibition and to modify the revolutionary tone of early Shi'ism to become a more sober and tolerant school of Islamic thought. The Shi'ite leaders encouraged, and even required, the use of prudent concealment *(taqiyya)* in the propagation of their faith so as to avoid pressing for the establishment of outright Shi'ite rule and the overthrow of the illegitimate caliphate. *Taqiyya*-oriented life also signified the will of the Shi'ite minority to continue to strive for the realization of the ideal by preparing the way for such an insurrection in the future.

Ja'far al-Sâdiq's contribution in shaping the religious and juridical direction of Shi'ism was central. All the Shi'ite factions acknowledged him as their imam, including those of radical leaning who led the revolts to establish descendants of 'Alî as legitimate heads of state. He was also recognized as an authentic transmitter of the traditions in the Sunni compilations. Under his leadership moderate Shi'ism, with its veneration of the Prophet's family, came to be recognized by the Sunni majority as a valid expression of personal piety. For the majority of Shi'ites his attitude toward politics became the cornerstone of their political theory, which, in the absence of the imam's political authority, did not teach its followers to overthrow tyrannical rulers and replace them by their imam. They had to wait for the messianic descendant from the "seed of the Prophet through his daughter Fâtima and grandson Husayn" to emerge as the Mahdî of the community. The doctrine of the imamate clarified the dilemma that although the imam was entitled to exercise comprehensive political authority as the head of the state, his imamate was not contingent upon his being invested as the political head. The imamate was seen more realistically as a spiritual and moral, rather than a political, office.

The mainstream Shi'ites continued to uphold the leadership of the descendants of 'Alî and Fâtima through Ja'far al-Sâdiq until the line reached the twelfth imam, believed to be in concealment until the end of time. This "Hidden" imam is regarded as the promised messianic Mahdî, whose return to launch the final revolution that will establish the kingdom of God on earth is awaited by his followers. By being hidden or in "occultation" *(ghayba)*, the imam is incognito, but nevertheless still physically present. Muslim eschatology describes in great detail the return of the Mahdî, as well as that of Jesus, who together usher in the Battle of Armageddon and the ultimate defeat of the antichrist *(Dajjâl)* and the victory of God's justice on earth. This school of Shi'ism is known as the Ithnâ 'Ashariyya, or "Twelvers." In the absence of the Hidden Imam, their religious scholars, the ayatollahs, fulfill the role of functional imams and, not unlike the Roman Catholic pope, lead the community in all its religious affairs. They form the majority of the Shi'ites in many parts of the world, mainly in Iran, Iraq, Lebanon, and Bahrain, and form substantial minorities in Afghanistan, Pakistan, and India.

Other Shi'ite Groups

The Shi'ite movement was represented by various leaders, all members of the Prophet Muhammad's clan (the Hâshimites), who represented different trends of thought. Whereas the mainstream followed the line of the twelve imams, others adhered to the imam who called for political action and an activist response to the unjust governments in power. The latter included an extremist trend in Shi'ism calling for the overthrow of Sunni dynasties. Mainstream Shi'ites condemned this trend, and over the course of history such minority factions have died out. Besides the Twelvers, the two factions that were once politically activist and have survived the vicissitudes of history are the Zaydîs and the Ismâ'îlîs. Their survival strategy, not unlike that in Iraq or in Lebanon today, has been to abandon political idealism, concentrating their opposition instead on spiritual and mystical paths. Until recently, however, Zaydîs, who are mainly to be found in Yemen and East Africa, believed that the imam ought to be a ruler of the state and therefore must fight for his rights.

The Ismâ'îlîs, so named after Ismâ'îl, the eldest son of Ja'far al-Sâdiq, who predeceased his father, believed that Ismâ'îl's son Muhammad was their seventh Imam. The number seven derives its symbolic religious significance in Isma'ili theology from this seventh Imam, who was also believed to be a messianic leader. The esoteric interpretation of the Qur'an, which was an overall heritage of all Shi'ites, found its sustained connection with this faction, earning them the title of Bâtiniyya (i.e., those who believe in the *bâtin* [hidden, inner] meanings of the Qur'an). After an initial dormant period in the movement's history, with three descendants of the seventh imam believed to be "concealed imams," Isma'ilis attained political and religious prominence under the Fâtimid dynasty (909-1171), which challenged the supremacy of the vast Sunni Abbasid caliphate.

The Ismâ'îlîs are divided today into two main branches: the Musta'lî (known as Bohoras) and the Nizârî (known as Aga Khânîs). The Bohoras trace their origins to Fâtimid religious missionaries in Yemen and continue much of the Fâtimid religious heritage under their present religious leader, who resides in India and who, as the "Absolute Guide" *(dâ'î al-mutlaq)*, is the representative of the twenty-first, hidden Fâtimid imam. Outside India they are found principally along the Indian Ocean littoral and in Pakistan, Tajikistan, Iran, Syria, and also in the United Kingdom, Canada, and the United States. The Aga Khânîs trace their origins to Iran, where their leaders had established the religious order. The Imam — known widely as the Aga Khân (from the title bestowed on him by the Qajars) but known to his followers as *hâzar imâm,* "the present imam" (as opposed to *ghâ'ib imâm,* "the hidden imam") — moved in the nineteenth century to Bombay. The Aga Khânî community is concentrated in central Asia, Iran, East Africa, Pakistan, and India, with significant communities in North America and western Europe. The present Aga Khân is based in France.

Suffering, Martyrdom, and Shrine Culture

As a minority community, Shi'ites suffered oppression under the majority Sunni dynasties throughout much of their history, especially under the Ghaznavids (975-1187), the Seljuks (1037-1194), the Zengids (1127-1250), the Ayyûbids (1171-1341), the Mamlûks (1250-1517), and the Ottomans (1517-1924), whose rule reduced the spread of Shi'ism in many areas, eradicating it in all of Egypt and in many Syrian cities (e.g., Aleppo), and confining

Shi'ites to remote areas. There were times, however, such as during the tenth and eleventh centuries, called by some the "Shi'ite century," when Shi'ite dynasties were politically ascendant, controlling large parts of the Muslim empire: the Buwayhids (934-1062) in Iran and Iraq; the Fâtimids (909-1171) in Egypt, Syria, the Hijâz, and for a time Tunisia and Sicily; and the Hamdânids in Aleppo (944-1015). In the sixteenth century, Safavid Iran (1502-1736) adopted Shi'ism as the official state religion.

Martyrdom *(shahâda)* became a religious factor in Shi'ite political history, sustained by a doctrine that God is just and commands human society to replace an unjust rule by a just and legitimate one. The ensuing struggle to install a legitimate political authority resulted in the murder of several Shi'ite leaders. These violent deaths were regarded by succeeding generations as martyrdom suffered in order to defeat the forces of oppression and falsehood.

The most powerful symbol of martyrdom is the third Shi'ite imam, Husayn (d. 680), Muhammad's grandson and 'Ali's son, whose martyrdom is annually commemorated with mourning throughout the Shi'ite world during the rites of Ashura (*'âshûra,* from *'ashara,* "ten"). In Karbala (in present-day Iraq) on the tenth day of the month of Muharram, Husayn and his family and followers were mercilessly killed by Umayyad troops. The Shi'ites have preserved this moment in their religious history as a tragic event reminding them of the corrupt nature of power and the way the righteous suffer. For the greater part of Shi'ite history, the memory of the tragedy of Karbala has been tempered by the tradition of political quietism; at times, however, the episode has encouraged activism to counter injustice in society.

The commemoration of the tragedy has served as a principal platform of communication with the Shi'ite public, and through it leaders such as Ayatollahs Khomeini (d. 1989) and Muhammad Bâqir al-Sadr (d. 1980) have disseminated sociopolitical and religious ideas. It has also become, for instance in Lebanon and Iraq, a model in the struggle to improve the standing and increase the influence of the Shi'ite population in those countries. In contrast to Sunnism, in Shi'ism special buildings constructed for the purpose of such commemoration, the Husayniyya, have served as crucial centers for public religious education and mourning rituals. Besides the *madrasas* (seminaries), the religious leaders used the Husayniyyas to disseminate either an activist or quietist ideology for their followers. The Iranian revolution in 1978-79 used the Karbala paradigm to mobilize the people against the corrupt rule of the Shah of Iran.

Closely related to martyrdom in Shi'ism was the shrine culture encouraged by the religious practice of a visit *(ziyâra)* to a *mashhad* (place where a martyr died and is buried, i.e., a shrine). In Shi'ite piety all imams are revered as martyrs, and their tombs are visited in the belief that such a devotional act will win forgiveness of sins and a share in the final victory of the messianic Imâm al-Mahdî. The tombs visited include those of both male and female members of the Prophet's family. In Iraq and Iran, for instance, it is common for both Shi'ites and Sunnis to undertake these pilgrimages. These shrines are richly endowed, and various Muslim rulers, especially members of Shi'ite dynasties, bestow lavish gifts. Towns have grown up around them, and important centers of Shi'ite learning exist in and around the shrines in Najaf, Iraq, and in Qom and Mashhad, Iran.

Shi'ite Theology and Jurisprudence

Shi'ism holds five fundamental principles or beliefs: (1) the unity of God, (2) the justice of God, (3) prophecy, (4) the imamate, and (5) the Day of Judgment. On every tenet but the fourth, Shi'ites in general share common ground with Sunnis, although there are differences on points of detail. The belief in the justice of God, for example, is similar to that of the Sunni Mu'tazilîs, rationalist theologians who were active from the eighth to the tenth century, when they were eclipsed by the traditionalist Sunni theologians known as the Ash'arîs (see "Islamic Philosophy," chapter 6). In the ninth and tenth centuries, when the theological exposition of the Shi'ite school was being worked out, its theologians adopted an essentially rational theology in which reason was prior to both sources of revelation, the Qur'an and the Sunna (see "Hadith and Sunna," chapter 4). Reason is God's endowment for humanity. It guides a person to ethical knowledge and asserts that good and evil are rational categories, independent of whether revelation declares them as such. While belief in the imamate is not a fundamental principle of religion for Sunnis, for Shi'ites it is the central and cardinal principle.

In accord with its rational theology, Shi'ite jurisprudence confers priority on reason. The comprehensiveness of Islamic revelation must be discovered, interpreted, and applied by use of reason. Accordingly, in their legal theory Shi'ites include reason as a fourth source of authority in deducing rulings of the Shari'a, in addition to the Qur'an, the Sunna, and the consensus *(ijmâ')* of jurists, which Sunni legal scholars accept. Not just anyone, however, can undertake the interpretation of the scriptural sources rationally. Only a religiously qualified person can assume the authority that accrues to the imam as the rightful successor of the Prophet. This authority in Shi'ism is invested in a jurist *(mujtahid)* who applies his independent reasoning in issuing a judicial decision *(fatwâ)*. Moreover, Shi'ites include the communications of their imams as part of the Sunna. Although the Shi'ite Sunna differs only in minor ways from the Sunna accepted by Sunnis, Shi'ites have their own compilations of Prophetic traditions. And although Shi'ites have been developing their religious-legal practice ever since the Middle Ages — themselves having founded al-Azhar in Cairo in 975, the oldest seminary (now a university) in a majority Muslim part of the world — only recently have some Sunni scholars come formally to acknowledge the validity of this practice.

Chapter Nine

SUNNIS, SUNNISM

Scott C. Lucas

Term

"Sunni" is an abbreviation of the Arabic *ahl al-sunna*, "the people of the Sunna" (literally "custom," "way"), that is, the people who follow the exemplary practice of the Prophet Muhammad. The phrase is itself an abbreviation of *ahl al-sunna wal-jamâ'a*, "the people of the Sunna and the community"; the term "Sunnism" is the resulting Anglicization. Because the vast majority of Muslims have always been Sunnis — nearly all sectarian groups, with the exception of the main body of Shi'ites, having dwindled to relatively small numbers or become extinct — "Sunni" has been synonymous with "Muslim" in most Muslim areas. The consolidation of Sunni Islam can be credited to several major developments within Islam: the establishment of the caliphate, the canonization of hadith collections, the formation of legal schools and of law colleges, the consolidation of spiritual and mystical practices and the institution of Sufi orders, and the rise of schools of speculative theology.

The Caliphate *(Khalîfa)*

The caliphate is a system of government at whose head is the caliph *(khalîfa)*, or vicegerent of God on earth (see "Islamic Government," chapter 11). From its humble origins after the death of Muhammad in 632, when Abû-Bakr (d. 634) was acclaimed caliph, the caliphate grew rapidly in stature. During the caliphates of ʿUmar (d. 644) and ʿUthmân (d. 656), the Muslims conquered Egypt, Syria, Iraq, and Iran. ʿUthmân was succeeded by Muhammad's cousin and son-in-law, ʿAlî (d. 661). These four leaders, whom Sunnis call "rightly guided caliphs" *(al-khulafâ' al-râshidûn)*, occupy a hallowed status in the formation of Sunni dogma. Sunnis historically remained loyal to the caliph, regardless of his personal qualities or behavior. ʿAlî's successor (and opponent), the caliph Muʿâwiya (ruled 661-680, d. 680), founded a dynasty called the Umayyads (661-750) and is credited in the Sunni tradition with permanently transforming the caliphate into a hereditary kingship.

The longest-lasting caliphate was that of the Abbasids (750-1258), who seized power from the Umayyads in 750 and wielded real political power from their capital in Baghdad (and its environs) until the early 900s. By 945 the caliph had lost all political power but retained symbolic prestige among Sunnis, which lasted long beyond the infamous Mongol sack of Baghdad in 1258. This prestige derived from the sterling reputations of the first caliphs and the Sunni ideal of a unified Muslim community under a single ruler. A new line of purely ceremonial Abbasid caliphs was supported by the staunchly Sunni rulers of Egypt almost immediately after the catastrophic events of 1258.

The final Ottoman sultans also adopted the title of caliph to bolster their support from Sunnis worldwide. Mustafa Kemal Atatürk (d. 1938) officially abolished that caliphate in 1924; one interesting consequence of this decision was the rise of a caliphate movement in far-off India in the early twentieth century in support of the Ottomans. At least one contemporary Sunni political organization, Hizb al-Tahrîr (the "Party of Liberation"), has as its central platform the restoration of this institution.

Hadith Collections

In the ninth and tenth centuries, scholars of Hadith produced over a dozen large volumes that recorded the teachings of the Prophet Muhammad, his Companions *(Sahâba),* their successors *(tâbiʿîn),* and other early pious figures, and assessed the reliability of hundreds of transmitters of this material. The figure of the Prophet was at the center of these efforts, and in a very short time such collections came to focus exclusively on his teachings. (See "Hadith and Sunna," chapter 4.)

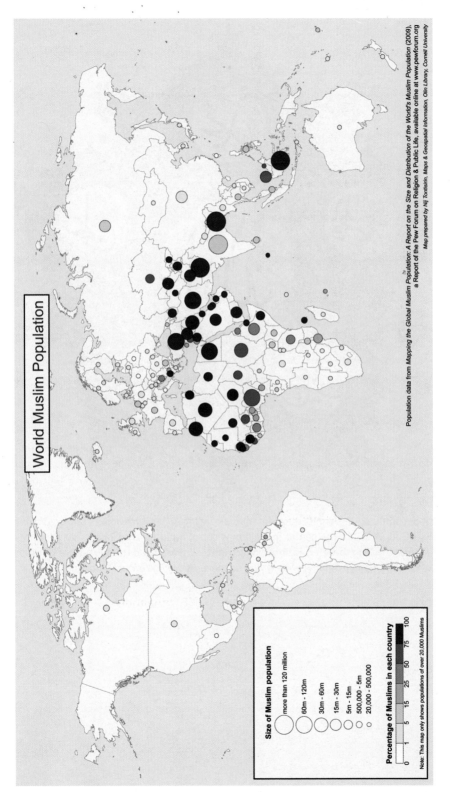

Population data from *Mapping the Global Muslim Population: A Report on the Size and Distribution of the World's Muslim Population* (2009), a Report of the Pew Forum on Religion & Public Life, available online at www.pewforum.org

Map prepared by Nij Tontisirin, Maps & Geospatial Information, Olin Library, Cornell University

World Muslim Population

Size of Muslim population

- more than 120 million
- 60m - 120m
- 30m - 60m
- 15m - 30m
- 5m - 15m
- 500,000 - 5m
- 20,000 - 500,000

Percentage of Muslims in each country

0   1   5   15   25   50   75   100

Note: This map only shows populations of over 20,000 Muslims

Fig. 1. Map of world Muslim population

Fig. 2. A decorative calligraphic representation of the Prophet Muhammad's family *(ahl al-bayt)*. The word God *(Allâh)* in the center medallion is surrounded by their names. At the top is the name Muhammad, on the left is Fâtima, on the right ʿAlî; Hasan and Husayn appear bottom right and bottom left. *(Public domain photograph accessed through Wikimedia Commons)*

Fig. 3. Haji Ali Dargah (built 1431) on an islet off Worli in Mumbai, India. This tomb-shrine and mosque is visited and venerated by Muslims and non-Muslims alike. *(Photograph courtesy of Dr. David Toorawa)*

Fig. 4. The Al-Farooq Mosque (built 1980), in Home Park, Atlanta, Georgia. Since 1994, the building includes a school and seminary. The Muslim population of Atlanta, which includes American Muslims and Muslims from 50 countries, is estimated at 75,000. *(Public domain photograph by Chris Yunker, accessed through Wikimedia Commons)*

Fig. 5. Interior of the Niujie Mosque, in the Xuanwu District of Beijing, China. First built in 996, and enlarged under the Qing Emperor Kangxi (d. 1722), it is Beijing's oldest and largest mosque. *(Photograph courtesy of Saqib Hasan)*

Fig. 6. The Great Mosque, Djenné, Mali. This is the largest mud brick or adobe building in the world. The first mosque on this site was built in the 13th century, but this structure dates from 1907. It is a UNESCO-designated World Heritage Site. *(Public domain photograph by Ruud Zwart, accessed through Wikimedia Commons)*

Fig. 7. Persian miniature, page from the *Khamsa* of Nizâmî (housed in the British Museum), mid-16th century, depicting the Miʿrâj, or Ascent, of the Prophet Muhammad to Paradise. He is seated on the fantastic steed, al-Burâq, led by Gabriel, and surrounded by other angels. *(Public domain photograph, accessed through Wikimedia Commons)*

Fig. 8. Mural on the house of a Hâjjî (someone who has performed the Hajj pilgrimage), near Luxor, southern Egypt. Such paintings by Egyptian pilgrims of modest means are quite common. *(Public domain photograph by Dr. Meierhofer, accessed through Wikimedia Commons)*

Fig. 9. The Ka'ba in the Grand Mosque, Mecca, Saudi Arabia. The Ka'ba is ritually circumambulated by pilgrims. The cubical stone structure is said to stand on the spot where Abraham built a shrine to God. *(Public domain photograph by Mardetanha, accessed through Wikimedia Commons)*

Fig. 10. The Prophet's Mosque, Medina, Saudi Arabia. Initially a small structure outside the Prophet Muhammad's home (currently beneath the green dome, where he is also buried), the enlarged mosque now accommodates over a million worshipers. *(Public domain photograph by Ali Mansuri, accessed through Wikimedia Commons)*

Fig. 11. Boys learning Arabic and Qur'an in Mauritania. Students practice lettering on wooden tablets. *(Public domain photograph by Ferdinand Reus, accessed through Wikimedia Commons)*

Fig. 12. Young women participating in a Silk & Spice festival, in front of the 16th-century Kalon Mosque, Bukhara, Uzbekistan. *(Public domain photograph by Yves Picq, accessed through Wikimedia Commons)*

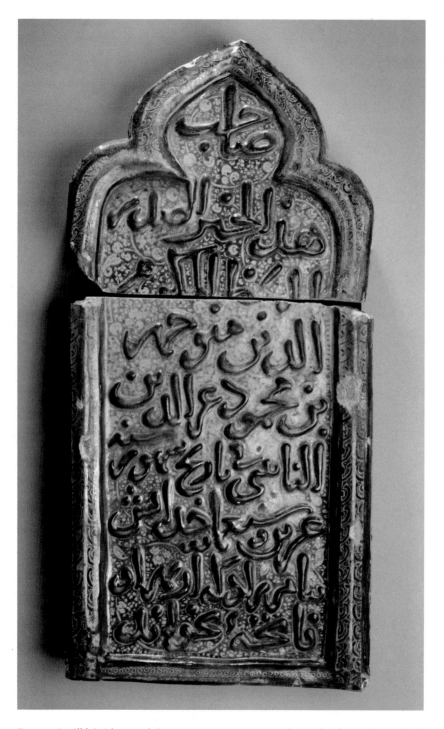

Fig. 13. An Ilkhânid period Persian commemorative tile in the form of a *mihrâb* (prayer niche), Kashan, Iran, 1320. Fritware with alkaline glazes. George and Mary Rockwell Fund, 2002.183 a,b. *(Photography courtesy of the Herbert F. Johnson Museum of Art, Cornell University)*

Fig. 14. Page from the Persian *Tarikh-i Jahan Gushay* ("History of the World Conqueror") depicting a battle between the conquering Mongols and the Muslim population of Iran. Opaque watercolors and gold on paper, Shiraz, atelier of Ibrâhîm Sultân ibn Shâh Rukh. George and Mary Rockwell Fund, 2005.024. *(Photography courtesy of the Herbert F. Johnson Museum of Art, Cornell University)*

Fig. 15. Painting of a youth holding an incense burner. Opaque watercolors and gold on paper, ca. 1640, Iran. The artist is unknown but the style is close to that of Muhammad Yûsuf a-Husaynî, the student of the acknowledged master of the genre, Rizâ Abbâsî (died 1635). George and Mary Rockwell Fund, 2002.009.001. *(Photography courtesy of the Herbert F. Johnson Museum of Art, Cornell University)*

Fig. 16. Page from a Judeo-Persian manuscript illustrating the biblical Jacob. Artist and date unknown, but probably 16th century. Judeo-Persian is Persian written in Hebrew script. Private collection of Susan and David Owen. *(Photography courtesy of Laura Johnson-Kelly)*

Legal Schools

Legal schools *(madhhabs)* coalesced around the teachings of prominent jurists, notably Abû-Hanîfa (d. 767), Mâlik-ibn-Anas (d. ca. 795), al-Shâfi'î (d. 820), and Ahmad-ibn-Hanbal (d. 855). The four schools that take their names from these four jurists — Hanafî, Mâlikî, Shâfi'î, and Hanbalî — developed distinctive bodies of legal doctrine, established individual legal methodologies, attracted deeply loyal followers, and have collectively maintained their privileged positions as the sole surviving Sunni schools of law until this day. Prominent jurists whose schools did not survive include Sufyân al-Thawrî (d. 778), Ibn-Râhawayh (d. ca. 853), Dâwûd al-Zâhirî (d. ca. 884), and al-Tabarî (d. 923). By the fourteenth century, most Sunnis belonged to one of the four legal schools, were affiliated with one of three theological schools (see below), and were initiated into any number of Sufi brotherhoods. In many parts of the Muslim empire, the choice of legal school would be largely predetermined by geography. For example, in Sumatra and Java, one would be a Shâfi'î, whereas in Mali one would almost certainly be a Mâlikî. This pattern continued largely uninterrupted until the arrival of European imperial powers, which, by the First World War, occupied most of the lands in which Sunni Muslims were a majority of the population, from Senegal to what is today Indonesia.

Law Colleges

The law college, or *madrasa* (literally "place of study"), appears to have emerged with the arrival of the Seljuk Turks in northeastern Persia, starting in the mid–eleventh century, and spread rapidly throughout the entire Middle East. All four Sunni schools of law succeeded in establishing independent *madrasas*, although it became common for patrons to endow legal colleges in which jurists from all four schools taught. The *madrasa* was the heart of the classical Muslim educational system, replete with endowed professorships for Arabic grammar, Islamic law, and, in due time, additional religious disciplines of legal theory, theology, and Hadith studies. The introduction of European educational and political institutions in largely Muslim areas, in particular the arrival of European missionary schools in the nineteenth century, severely undermined the *madrasa*. Today, the term *madrasa* is used more commonly to refer to primary and secondary schools than colleges.

Dialectical Theology *(Kalâm)*

Several schools of theology (*'ilm al-kalâm*, literally "the science of dialectical [or speculative] theology") emerged over the course of the ninth and tenth centuries, the most important of which were the Mu'tazilî, the Ash'arî, and the Mâturîdî, the last two grounded in the writings of their eponyms, al-Ash'arî (d. 935) and al-Mâturîdî (d. ca. 944) (see "Islamic Philosophy," chapter 6). Many scholar-theologians of the Hadith insisted upon the curtailment of speculative theology beyond the literal word of the Qur'an and Hadith, arguing for instance that debate about the status of the divine attributes was forbidden. This anti-*kalâm* position was something of a school of theology itself.

Sunni theologians as a rule affirm a plurality of attributes by which God describes Himself in the Qur'an and Hadith. Hadith-scholar theologians affirm all of God's attributes and reject interpreting them or reducing them to a specific number. Ash'arî theologians regularly restrict the number of eternal attributes that are "neither God nor other than God" to seven: knowledge, power, life, will, seeing, hearing, and speech. Adherents of the Mâturîdî school, such as al-Nasafî (d. ca. 1142), identify additional divine attributes beyond the "Ash'arî seven," such as creating, desiring, doing, and sustaining. An important hallmark of Sunni theology concerning the divine attributes is the insistence that the Qur'an is the eternal speech of God and cannot be considered to have been created at any point in time, in contradistinction to the Mu'tazili insistence on God's unity and the Qur'an's consequent createdness.

Unlike the Mu'tazilîs and most Shi'ites, who believed humans created their own actions, Sunni theologians argued that certain Qur'anic verses, such as "He created all things" and "there is no God but He, Creator of all things" (Q 6:101-2), did not allow for the possibility of any rival creators to God. Despite their firm belief that humans cannot create their own acts without divine intervention, the Sunni theologians devised theories stipulating that human beings bear complete responsibility for their voluntary actions. These theories can be seen as defensive efforts against the accusations issued by Mu'tazilîs and Shi'ites that Sunnis had in fact stripped humans of all responsibility for their actions.

Another major topic stressed in Sunni doctrine from the earliest days was the affirmation that the historical sequence of the first four caliphs corresponds to their respective merits. In other words, Abû-Bakr was the greatest Muslim after Muhammad, followed by 'Umar, then 'Uthmân, and then 'Alî. Anyone who advocated that 'Alî was the most elevated Muslim after the Prophet was declared by Sunni religious authorities to be a de facto Shi'ite (a partisan of 'Alî, from *shî'at 'Alî*, "the party of 'Alî"). Sunnis also enforced categorically the principle that, in the words of al-Nasafî, "only good should be spoken about the Companions of Muhammad." The treatment of the Companions of Muhammad is probably the most acrimonious difference between Sunnis and Shi'ites, since Shi'ites degrade (and at times ritually curse) the majority of Muhammad's Companions for their failure to recognize 'Alî's claim to religio-political authority immediately following the death of Muhammad. By contrast, Sunnis venerate the Companions for their proximity to Muhammad and for their key role in understanding, implementing, and transmitting his teachings in the form of Hadith.

Sufism *(Tasawwuf)*

The early centuries of Islam witnessed a strengthening of ascetic, spiritual, and, eventually, mystical practices, or (what has come to be called) Sufism, and many of the famous early masters who came to be identified as Sufis, such as al-Muhâsibî (d. ca. 857) and al-Junayd (d. 910), were squarely in the Sunni fold (see "Sufism," chapter 7). During the twelfth and thirteenth centuries, Sufi brotherhoods and orders *(turuq)* emerged (though some groups had Shi'ite tendencies). Major transregional orders were based upon the spiritual exercises and teachings of such charismatic teachers as 'Abd al-Qâdir al-Jîlânî (d. 1166), al-Shâdhilî (d. 1258) in Morocco, and Mu'în-al-dîn al-Chishtî (d. 1236). These orders, which emerged all over the Muslim empire, rapidly developed the institutional structure of the *khânqâh*, or Sufi lodge, which soon became a regular fixture in Muslim society. The popular veneration of saints *(awliyâ', "friends [of God]")* grew alongside the high literary tradition of the Sufi orders, and soon shrines or tombs became ubiquitous. The rapid rise of secular nationalism and Salafi Islamism among Sunnis in the early twentieth century (see below), however, significantly challenged the esoteric metaphysics and practices of many of the established mystical orders.

Modern Developments

The key catalysts of change within Islam in the past five centuries were the increasing institutionalization of the Ottoman Empire; the spread of Islam in West Africa, South Asia, and Southeast Asia; and the rise of European powers, which ultimately conquered much of the Muslim empire. Although European interference played a major role in Sunni developments, especially over the past two centuries, it is clear that a purely internal reorientation appeared in the eighteenth century. Scholars such as Shâh Walî Allâh (d. 1762) in India, Muhammad Ibn-ʿAbd-al-Wahhâb (d. 1792) in Arabia, and al-Shawkânî (d. 1834) in Yemen challenged prevailing theological and even legal paradigms in unique ways.

One methodology common to many of these scholars entailed a new emphasis on the study of the Hadith and the opinions of the earliest authorities in Islam, known as the *salaf* (literally "early [Muslims]"). This reevaluation of the tradition is often described as Salafi Islam, an expression that has become confusing because of its application both to Sunnis perceived of as being liberal, such as the Egyptian Muhammad ʿAbduh (d. 1905), and to those considered ultraconservative and literalist, such as the Wahhâbîs of the modern kingdom of Saudi Arabia. The term also refers on occasion to the Hanbalî school, which historically emphasized Hadith, discouraged speculative theology, and produced some of the heroes of Salafi Islam, such as Ibn-Taymiyya (d. 1328) and Ibn-ʿAbd-al-Wahhâb. It is also applied at times to twentieth-century sociopolitical organizations, such as the Muslim Brotherhood, that declare Islam to be a comprehensive ideology that is the only solution for a litany of modern Muslim problems, including tyranny, inequality, corruption, and political impotence. The most well-known ideologue of the Muslim Brotherhood remains Sayyid Qutb, who was executed by President Nasser of Egypt in 1966.

One prominent theme in twentieth- and twenty-first-century Sunni discourse has been reform. Numerous Western-educated Muslim scholars and intellectuals have called for a reassessment of the inherited tradition, especially in the legal sphere. Major writers in this vein include the South Asian Muhammad Iqbâl (d. 1938), the Indonesian Nurcholish Madjid (d. 2005), the Algerian Mohamed Arkoun (d. 2010), the Syrian Muhammad Shahrour, the Moroccan Fatima Mernissi, the Swiss-Egyptian Tariq Ramadan, and the African-American Sherman Jackson.

While the ideas of reformers and ideologues are certainly significant, the vast majority of observant Sunnis should probably be classified as traditional Muslims who endeavor to harmonize inherited beliefs and practices with modern social and economic realities. Institutions located in the sphere of traditional Sunnism range from al-Azhar University in Cairo to the Nahdatul Ulama (Renaissance of Islamic Scholars) in Indonesia, the world's largest Muslim organization. Since most efforts to "Islamize" society from above have had very limited success, it seems safe to say that the future of Sunni Islam will largely be determined by the vast community of traditional believers across the globe whose daily interactions with contemporary ideas and practices ensure the continuing vitality of this 1,400-year-old tradition.

PART IV

INSTITUTIONS

Chapter Ten

MOSQUE

Ruba Kana'an

Term

For Muslims, prayer takes on many forms and expressions, and Muslims have developed and used a range of spaces for worship and devotion. Ritual prayer is performed individually, and communally, in locations ranging from the privacy of the home to places of gathering, places of learning, mausoleums, and even open spaces. Despite this variety, the *masjid*, or mosque, has come to be the main place for ritual prayer. A *masjid* (literally "place of prostration") is generally any place where Muslims perform communal ritual prayer (which the Prophet Muhammad described as "superior to individual prayer by twenty-seven degrees"). The word *masjid* occurs several times in the Qur'an, referring to the Ka'ba in Mecca (*al-Masjid al-Harâm*), possibly to the Aqsa mosque in Jerusalem (*al-Masjid al-Aqsâ*, "furthest mosque"), and also to the building erected over the tomb of the Seven Sleepers (Q 18:21). This suggests that the word was also used for any place where God is worshiped, and later came to be specifically used as the main word for the place where Muslims perform their ritual prayers. *Masjid* does not denote an architectural shape, form, size, or content; that is, there are no specific spatial requirements beyond the orientation toward the Ka'ba in Mecca (the *qibla*).

The Prophet's Mosque

Muslim ritual prayer gained its form and structure during the lifetime of Prophet Muhammad. A number of mosques were also established during the same period. The most significant amongst these was the mosque built at Medina in the year 622-23 where the Prophet led the prayers and established and developed the early Muslim community. The Prophet's mosque no longer survives in its original form, as it has been continuously rebuilt and expanded to accommodate the increasing number of worshipers, starting from the reign of the second caliph, 'Umar, in 638 up to its most recent expansion in 1997. Historical reconstructions of the Prophet's original mosque in Medina are based on early literary sources, which suggest that the mosque was an enclosure with a covered area in the direction of prayer toward Mecca opening onto a courtyard surrounded by arcades. The mosque in Medina served as a place of prayer and a communal place where the Prophet addressed issues concerning the early community. There are numerous references in Hadith literature about the different sorts of activities that took place in the Prophet's mosque, including gathering of people, political negotiations, lounging, and sleeping. The Prophet's mosque thus also served as a political, administrative, and community center. The private residences of the Prophet and his wives were adjacent to the mosque enclosure but mostly outside the space or separated from it.

Historical evidence suggests that the idea of the arcaded prayer hall and courtyard surrounded by arcades in the Prophet's mosque at Medina was used for the construction of later mosques. This architectural composition can be seen in an early Umayyad mosque built in Wâsit, Iraq, in 703, the earliest mosque for which there is secure archaeological evidence. Despite the prominence of the arcaded prayer hall and courtyard, this architectural form served as a guiding principle rather than an architectural model; local building traditions and techniques played a significant role in the architectural articulation of mosque forms, resulting in a whole range of styles of mosque types.

Types of Mosques

Historically, four main types of mosques can be identified, though in many places a single mosque satisfied all functions. The majority of mosques are neighborhood ones, established for the practical use of worshipers for everyday prayer. In some places, such as big cities, neighborhood mosques were built at regular intervals to accommodate dense populations. Friday prayers are performed in the congregational mosque *(jâmi')*. According to some Muslim traditions, the difference between everyday prayers and the Friday prayers is that, although both are obligatory for all adult men, the Friday prayer should be performed in the mosque along with other Muslims. These early afternoon Friday prayers are also followed by a sermon that is delivered from the pulpit *(minbar)*. Most surviving historic monumental mosques were Friday mosques, as they were an obvious location for founders to demonstrate their piety and magnanimity through lavish design and decoration. A third type of mosque, known in Arabic as *musallâ* and in Urdu as *'Îd-gâh* or *namâz-gâh*, meaning simply "a place for prayer," is used during religious festivals such as the two high holidays (the Feast of Fast-Breaking, marking the end of Ramadan, and the Feast of Sacrifice, at the end of the Hajj pilgrimage). Historically, these were large open spaces on the outskirts of urban settlements devoid of monumental superstructures. As for funerary or memorial mosques, these typically housed a place of prayer where mourners prayed for forgiveness for the deceased. The variety and complexity of places of burial and commemoration built by Muslims are quite impressive. Funerary mosques are usually part of grand imperial monuments set in elaborate landscapes, tomb complexes that are embedded within social and religious complexes, individual monuments, or necropolises.

Regional Styles of Mosque Architecture

As buildings, mosques developed in different shapes and forms according to the geographic regions in which they were built and in response to environmental factors, local building traditions, and stylistic developments. Historically, Muslims adapted local building traditions to the physical needs of Muslim ritual prayer, mainly the orientation toward Mecca. The Great Mosque of Djenné, built in Mali in 1907, for example, is built in the local domestic architectural technique of mud walls created from local earth supporting a flat roof of palm trunks. The Djenné mosque looks remarkably different from the sixteenth-century Süleymaniye mosque built in Istanbul in 1557. This stone-built mosque has a large central dome surrounded by a cascade of half-domes; the prayer hall is flanked with an open courtyard framed with four pencil-shaped minarets. The Süleymaniye is typical of Ottoman mosques, and its style is ultimately based on the Byzantine church of Hagia Sophia that was built by the Byzantine emperor Justinian in 532-537. When the Ottomans conquered Istanbul in 1453, they added a *mihrâb* (see below) to the existing church and turned it into a mosque. The adaptation of pre-Islamic religious building styles resulted in different mosque forms. The Great Mosque of Xian, built in China in the fourteenth century, for example, resembles Chinese Buddhist temples with its courtyards and pagodas arranged on a single axis; the main difference is the orientation of the prayer hall toward Mecca.

A specific visual language of mosque architecture based on domes and minarets is a late development that can be linked, in part, to the political and historical developments of scholarship on Islam. The project of classification and description led by Napoleon's *savants* in early-nineteenth-century Egypt and the French colonial officers in North Africa led, amongst other things, to the creation of a new field of knowledge known as "Islamic architecture." The Middle East with its specific building styles and practices came to define what Western scholarship perceived as "Islamic architecture" with domes and minarets as typical identifying features of a "Muslim" landscape. In the decades following the independence of the nations where Islam was the majority religion (the 1940s to 1960s), most of the newly formed states used mosque architecture as a way to create a symbolic language that marked the period of decolonization. The King Faisal mosque built 1970-1986 in Islamabad, Pakistan, for example, departed from the historical form of mosque common to the Indian subcontinent, and was built as a tentlike domical building surrounded by four minarets. The form of contemporary state-mosques from Indonesia to Morocco, as well as central mosques in Europe and North America, is perhaps one of the best examples of the invention of a building tradition where domed buildings with one or more minarets have come to be seen by Muslims and non-Muslims as symbols of Muslim identity.

Architectural Components of a Mosque

The architectural components that have regularly come to be identified with mosques include: the *mihrâb,* a marker for the direction of prayer; the minaret, a tower used for the call to prayer; and the *minbar,* a pulpit used for sermons. According to Muslim jurists, these elements are not essential for the performance of ritual prayer, nor are they required to qualify a building as a mosque. All that is required for ritual prayer is that the believers orient themselves toward the Ka'ba in Mecca. Muslims can perform prayers wherever they find themselves, including outdoors, in or on a moving vehicle, or, for the invalid, in bed.

The direction of Mecca is indicated by the *mihrâb*, usually, but not uniquely, rendered in the form of a niche in the center of the *qibla* wall facing the Ka'ba. A *mihrâb* can be flat, in the form of a concave niche, or a recessed room. It is usually the focus of architectural decoration in a mosque. The earliest reference to a *mihrâb* dates to the Umayyad reconstruction of the Prophet's mosque in Medina in 705. The incorporation of the *mihrâb* in mosque architecture, in particular its location in the position where the Prophet used to pray, suggests that the *mihrâb* may have stood in for the (absent) Prophet.

A minaret is traditionally the place from which the call to prayer *(adhân)* is announced. The minaret first evolved when Muslims used elevated buildings and rooftops to call adherents to prayer during the life of the Prophet. The earliest surviving minaret is part of the Great Mosque of Damascus built by the Umayyads in 705-715. Minarets come in many shapes and forms and are built with different materials. Historically, the most common type is a tower. In Syria and North Africa these tower minarets are square and made of stone or earth; in Turkey and South Asia they are cylindrical and typically made of stone; in Iran and central Asia they are also cylindrical but are made of brick and ceramic tile; and in Egypt they are multistory with different profiles and are made with a variety of materials. Mosques have also been built with different numbers of minarets. Indeed, in some regions like Oman and East Africa mosques often do not have tower minarets at all. In Iran and central Asia two minarets, flanking an arched recess or portal *(îwân)*, became common from the thirteenth century onward, whereas the Ottomans framed their mosques with two, four, or six minarets.

The *minbar* is the pulpit used to deliver religious sermons *(khutba)*, usually during the Friday prayer. Its most common form is a structure with a few steps and an elevated seat, with or without a hood. A less well-known type of *minbar* — a concave recess next to the *mihrâb* and sometimes connected to it — is common in East Africa and southern Arabia. The *minbar's* development is linked to a seat on which Prophet Muhammad used to stand when addressing his followers. It is thus linked to the Prophet's role as a religious and political leader. Historically *minbars* served as places for the prayer leader *(imâm)* to both deliver his sermon and lead the prayer, often in the name of the ruler or ruling dynasty. Historically, only the central Friday mosque of the main town in a province had a *minbar*. With time, they were introduced in the central mosques of each town before they eventually became a common feature in mosques.

The Building and Decoration of Mosques

The prerogative of the building and management of mosques has changed over time. Whereas the mosques of the early Islamic period were usually established to fulfill an immediate communal need, by the rulers or their representatives, the building of mosques — especially Friday mosques — saw a dramatic upturn from the early thirteenth century onward. Local governors, military leaders as well as private individuals, both male and female, started establishing multiple Friday mosques and managing their affairs. The discussion of who has the right to build a mosque or deliver the Friday sermon there occupied Muslim jurists and produced different responses. For example, in the Sunni tradition there was a single Friday Mosque *(jâmi')* in each city with a number of smaller mosques *(masjids)* in its different neighborhoods. With time, the four Sunni schools, especially the Hanafîs, accepted and justified the presence of several Friday mosques based on necessity due to the growth of the community. In the Ibâdi legal tradition dominant in Oman and southern Algeria, on the other hand, the number of historical Friday mosques is limited to the cities where their Imams resided.

Private individuals sought permission to establish mosques, yet they had no ownership rights over the buildings once they were completed. The creation of a religious endowment *(waqf)* was one of the most common ways a founder could establish some control over a mosque and its management. The religious endowment commonly consisted of revenue-generating properties given to the mosque in perpetuity. The founders retained the right to manage the endowment and appoint the mosque personnel, including the imam, who were paid from the revenue of the endowment. Mosques, typically, are not regarded as private property. The founders lose their property rights the first time prayers take place in the mosque. With the advent of nation-states in Muslim countries, the establishment and management of mosques became mostly institutionalized. The building of mosques and the management of all religious endowments have become the prerogative of a government department. These departments are responsible for issuing building permits with specific building regulations for mosques; they are also responsible for managing mosques as part of each country's "religious affairs."

Mosques are commonly decorated with calligraphic inscriptions, geometric patterns, and floral motifs. The written word remains the most important form of ornamentation in mosques. Calligraphic inscriptions comprising verses from the Qur'an or quotations from the Hadith are rendered in various forms and in different media. Inscriptions that mention the date of the building and the name and title of the mosque's founder are also placed in prominent locations. Decorative patterns are mostly placed at the structural divisions of the building — the base of the dome, the profile of an arch such as the *mihrâb,* or the frame of a recess. This applies both to the interior and to the exterior.

The copying and decoration of Qur'ans of different sizes and calligraphic styles were the traditional focus of mosque patronage. Qur'an boxes, Qur'an stands, and carved *minbars* were also commissioned for mosques. These objects were typically decorated with a combination of inscriptions, geometric interlace, and floral or vegetal motifs. The other major historical focus of patronage consisted of lighting fixtures in the form of candlesticks and hanging lamps. A common type of mosque lamp is the enameled and gilded glass lamp with a bulbous body and conical neck that can now be found in abundance in museum collections. These mosque lamps are for the most part inscribed with Qur'anic verses (especially the "Light verse," Q 24:35) and the names and titles of the patrons who commissioned them. Providing lighting for mosques necessitated the availability of a continuous supply of candles and oil as well as an employee whose job was to light and maintain the lamps and candles.

Women in the Mosque

The Qur'an does not differentiate between men's and women's obligation to pray to God. Muslim legal literature, however, came to identify particular areas where women's practice of prayer was distinguished from that of men. In particular the literature focuses on three concerns: when women can or cannot pray, what they need to wear when they pray, and their physical position in relationship to men during prayer. According to some legal scholars, women are not allowed to pray during menstruation as they are considered ritually impure. As a result, a menstruating woman was deemed unable to go into the mosque even if she was not praying. A second area of debate concerning women in mosques is their attire. Both men and women are required to cover their private parts ('awra) during the performance of prayer. The different schools of legal interpretation agree, with slight variations, that the whole of a woman's body should be covered during prayer, and hence when entering a mosque, except for the face, the palms, and the top of the feet. The type of cover required is left open to interpretation.

The position of women in relationship to men during prayer is also important and is closely linked to whether a woman can lead prayer — that is, be an imam — and hence pray in front of and be followed by men. There is a general consensus amongst scholars that being male is a condition for leading prayer, and most schools of interpretation agree that women can be imams only for other women. This position continues to be challenged, especially in contemporary Western contexts. With regard to prayer, however, scholars agree that women and men are not allowed to pray shoulder to shoulder. This general principle, however, is subject to broad interpretations that range from letting women pray side by side with men, or behind men and children. Most contemporary mosques reserve an area for women's prayer in the form of a separate room in the mosque or behind a physical barrier that separates men from women. Such segregated spaces continue to be contested by Muslim men and women alike, particularly in Western contexts. The juridical focus on the above-mentioned issues has led some Muslims to conclude that women are banned from mosques. While it is generally agreed that women, unlike men, are not obliged to perform the Friday prayer, there is no injunction on them entering or praying in a mosque. To the contrary, a Prophetic hadith explicitly asks men not to ban women from performing prayer in a mosque, except during menstruation.

Women have also been regular patrons of mosque architecture throughout Islamic history. By establishing religious endowments, women, like men, were able to use their own financial resources, and at times, political clout, to establish vast religious complexes that included mosques. As part of their prerogative as founders of waqf endowments, women maintained control of all the details of the building and management of the mosques and other properties covered by the endowment. Mosques and religious complexes founded by women continue to be known by the names of their female founders, such as the Mosque of Gawhar Shad in Herat in western Afghanistan, built 1417-1438 and maintained by Tamerlane's daughter-in-law.

Chapter Eleven

ISLAMIC GOVERNMENT

Joseph E. Lowry

The Qur'an, the holy scripture of Islam, does not advocate or describe a specific form of government. In general, it champions individual holders of religio-moral authority, many of whom are biblical prophets, and such persons are often portrayed as being at odds with a political or socioeconomic elite. Typically, such prophets bring a message from God to a community; the community and its leaders refuse to believe the message and God then destroys the community but lets the prophet and his followers survive. This pattern is repeated, with some variation, in Qur'anic depictions of Noah, Abraham, Moses, and others, including nonbiblical Arabian prophets. Sometimes the opposition is a mighty political figure, such as Pharaoh in the case of Moses; sometimes it is a more modest opponent, such as Abraham's father. This pattern of a prophetic warning, disbelief and/or disobedience by a recalcitrant community, and divine wrath and destruction is counterbalanced by the positive portrayal of other wielders of political authority, such as Joseph, David, and Solomon. Generally, however, the main depiction of authority and right in the Qur'an consists of prophet-figures speaking truth to power. This prophetic pattern corresponds in its main outlines to the traditional account of Muhammad's experience in Mecca between the time he began to receive the Qur'anic revelation and acquire followers in 610, and his migration *(hijra)* to Medina in 622. The ruling elite of Mecca opposed Muhammad because his message contained overt criticisms of the reigning socioeconomic and religious structures of power and authority. Only after his migration to Medina at the invitation of Medinan tribes who were in conflict and who requested his services as a mediator did Muhammad himself acquire political authority.

Muhammad at Medina

Before the rise of Islam most inhabitants of Arabia experienced political authority through tribal and kinship-based social structures. This was true for nomads, seminomads, settled agriculturalists, and those who lived in urban settlements. Thus, when Muhammad and his Meccan followers first came to Medina, although they came as a religious community, they related to Medinan society as a quasi-tribal structure, as can be seen in the so-called Constitution of Medina, a document (or series of documents) that spells out the legal relationship between Muhammad's followers (styled "the believers," *al-mu'minûn*) and various named tribal groupings native to Medina. The diverse Medinan polity described by this document, which comprises both Muhammad's followers and the other non-Muslim parties, is called an *umma,* a word that subsequently came to refer solely to the worldwide community of Muslims irrespective of political boundaries. The document itself governs the concerns typical of tribally organized Arabia: relations with other tribes, retaliation and compensation for personal injury or death, cooperation in matters of external defense, and so on. It mandates that disputes arising under it be referred "to God . . . and Muhammad." It also appears to recognize the right of both Jews and Muslims to practice their respective religions: "To the Jews their religion and to the Muslims their religion." This document has, however, exercised little influence on Islamic political thought until recently, and has been mostly of scholarly interest.

Muhammad's own political fortunes are noteworthy because he began so unpromisingly, with a somewhat power-unfriendly message (reinforced by the Qur'an), but came to enjoy conspicuous political and military success, and to rule over the nucleus of what would become the largest empire of late antiquity. These aspects of his legacy became paradigmatic in the following ways: his critique of unjust political and social orders remained a potent inspiration for reformers; his apparent seamless fusion of political and religious authority retained great power as part of a hallowed memory of the unity and attendant worldly success of the primeval Muslim community; and this same combined success, although remaining a mostly unattainable ideal, nonetheless provided a critical standard against which to measure any earthly government. The power of this model can be seen in the fact that even a writer working in the Hellenistic philosophical tradition such as al-Fârâbî (d. ca. 950) viewed prophetic government as paradigmatic and as akin to rule by Plato's philosopher-king. It is also worth noting that the model of the genesis of the Muslim community, involving a relatively rapid conquest of and rule over much of the known world, differs greatly from its Christian counterpart, and at least materially from its counterpart in ancient Judaism.

Sunnis

Muhammad made no provision for successors, but naturally he was succeeded upon his death (in 632) in his position as head of the Muslim polity. His successors were first called caliphs *(khulafâ', "successors"; sing. khalîfa)* — a Qur'anic term applied to Adam and King David, who are God's trustees on earth — and later "Commander of the Faithful" *(amîr al-mu'minîn)*. The so-called orthodox, or "rightly guided," caliphs ruled from Medina (632-661), the Umayyad caliphs from Damascus (661-750), and the Abbasid caliphs from Baghdad (750-1258). Sunnis came to recognize four rightly guided caliphs (Abû-Bakr, 'Umar, 'Uthmân, 'Alî) as Muhammad's legitimate successors, and their rule is remembered as a continuation of Muhammad's own success, but only the first of them died a natural death, the remaining three having been assassinated. The Umayyads, by contrast, were remembered as having wrested control from more deserving candidates, even though they seem to have made a strong bid for caliphal religious authority. They were in any event infamous for introducing dynastic succession into what was widely viewed as a meritocratic practice based on piety and proximity to Muhammad.

By the time of the Abbasids, caliphal authority came to be projected through elaborate court ceremony, perhaps modeled on that of the Sassanian empire, in a way that emphasized the caliph's cosmic importance. However, disputes, occasionally violent, over legitimacy of rule during the "rightly guided" and Umayyad periods led to theological speculation about the ruler's piety. Dissatisfaction with caliphal rule led to the articulation of norms, standards of pious conduct, sin, and criteria of salvation, and these became generalized and applicable to Muslims at large (e.g., as Islamic law). Those who engaged in such speculation emerged as the scholarly institution of the ulema (*'ulamâ', "scholars"*), whose own religious authority, over the course of the eighth and ninth centuries, came to rival and ultimately to eclipse that of the caliphs.

All the caliphs were rulers in fact until the mid–tenth century, when the Abbasid empire fragmented and the central Islamic lands came to be ruled in many cases by various central Asian groups. Still, the caliphs' importance continued to be recognized by Sunni political theorists such as al-Mâwardî (d. 1058) and jurist-theologians such as al-Ghazâlî (d. 1111). The Abbasid caliphate ended with the Mongol sack of Baghdad in 1258, though Abbasid descendants received recognition as figureheads, first in Egypt under the Mamlûks, and then briefly into the Ottoman period, at which point the Ottoman sultans assumed the title. The Ottomans, who ruled southeastern Europe and the Middle East (1293-1923), were a powerful, militarily and bureaucratically adept polity that increasingly exercised direct control over previously private religious institutions and as a result over religious scholars. The Ottoman sultans went so far as to promulgate their own legislation, and even embarked on a project to codify Islamic law in the mid–nineteenth century. Such developments represented a technological advance in the art of governance, since private religious institutions had previously filled gaps of various kinds that were left open by inherent weaknesses in the structures of premodern states.

The central Asian military elites who ruled much of the Islamic empire in postcaliphal and pre-Ottoman times enhanced their political legitimacy by supporting private religious institutions and through them religious scholars, thus forging ties with local civilian elites and other constituencies. North Africa developed a distinctive regional variation of this pattern whereby scholarly elites would often withdraw to rural enclaves of religious and intellectual activity and thus form a counterbalance to urban-based political authority. This dialectic between rural and urban social structures, and the political ramifications of this, were elaborated in great detail by the philosopher and historian Ibn-Khaldûn (d. 1406) in his celebrated work, *The Prolegomenon.*

The replacement of the caliphs' religious authority by that of the ulema, who emphasized the simultaneous momentousness and remoteness of the golden age of Muhammad and the rightly guided caliphs, has presented a structural barrier to the realization of theocratic government in Sunni Islam, if not always to the yearning for it (including among some contemporary supporters of armed *jihâd*). One early movement, the seventh-century Khârijites, made the entire community charismatic and every member potentially suitable to rule but excluded sinners, making their property and lives forfeit and their families subject to enslavement. Although the early Sunnis were less militant than the Khârijites, the Khârijite example illustrates how the diffusion of authority, as among the Sunni ulema, could lead to a certain egalitarianism.

There have been exceptions, however, to the general Sunni reluctance to welcome charismatic rule, such as the Almoravids (1062-1147) and especially the Almohads (1130-1269) in Spain and North Africa and, in the nineteenth century, the caliphs of Sokoto (northern Nigeria and the Niger valley) and the revolt of the Mahdî (*mahdî*, literally, "rightly guided one," but actually a Messiah figure) against British rule in the Sudan (1880s-1890s). Also, both Morocco and Jordan remain monarchies whose rulers claim descent from the Prophet's family, though in both cases the associated claim of charisma, while more than implicit, is relatively modest (less so in Morocco), and religious authority remains firmly lodged with the ulema. Mustafa Kemal Atatürk (d. 1938) ultimately abolished the office of caliph in 1924 in connection with the founding of the Turkish Republic.

Shi'ites

For Shi'ites, matters were different. They held that the wrong persons had succeeded to the caliphate after Muhammad, and they thus formed and clung to a utopian ideal of the ruler, called an Imam (*imâm*, "leader," a term also used by Sunnis for the caliphs), who combined absolute political and religious authority. 'Alî-ibn-Abî-Tâlib (d. 661), Muhammad's cousin and son-in-law, was the fourth of the Sunnis' "rightly guided" caliphs, but the Shi'ites consider him their first Imam and believe that his immediate succession to Muhammad had been divinely decreed and expressly confirmed by Muhammad. The imams who succeeded 'Alî were held to be descended from him and Muhammad's daughter Fâtima (Muhammad had no sons). The Shi'ite imams enjoyed, in theory, a more robust connection to the supernatural than did the Sunni caliphs. Various Shi'ite groups achieved political power and formed states governed by Imams, the most important of which were the Fâtimids (909-1171) and the Safavids (1501-1736). The Fâtimids (named after Muhammad's daughter) came to power in North Africa in the ninth century, founded Cairo in the late tenth century, and ruled Egypt and Syria-Palestine until the late twelfth century as the main rivals to the Abbasid caliphs. Among their various offshoots today are the followers of the Aga Khân and the Dâwûdi Bohoras.

A messianic movement that came to power in Iran in 1500 led to the founding of the Safavid state, which patronized Imâmî (Twelver) Shi'ite ulema. When the state crumbled in 1722, the structure of scholarly authority remained and gradually evolved into that of modern Imâmi Shi'ism, more hierarchical than that of the Sunni ulema but still characterized by the diffusion of authority. The earthly failure of the Imâmi Shi'ite ideal of the charismatic ruler, where the advent of the true Imam was postponed until the end of time, left the Shi'ites in some ways freer to experiment than the Sunnis. In 2010, the closest thing to an Islamic theocracy is the Islamic Republic of Iran, which presents a fascinating mix of clerical and democratic rule. Its eclecticism is already foreshadowed in the political writings of the architect of the Islamic revolution in Iran, Ayatollah Khomeini (d. 1989), who held that only religious scholars were entitled to rule an Islamic state.

Prospects

Although the Safavids, who converted Iran to Shi'ism, were a self-consciously Shi'ite state in frequent conflict with the Ottomans, and the Ottoman sultans styled themselves as protectors of Sunnis everywhere, these two states, as well as the Mughals in India (1526-1858), laid great emphasis on the figure of the ruler (not unlike their European counterparts in England, France, and Austro-Hungary). Religious authority was thus only one part of a complex projection of legitimacy, and while this legitimacy was closely tied to Twelver Shi'ism for the Safavids, it was perhaps slightly less exclusively religious for the Ottomans and the Mughals, whose territories included substantial non-Muslim populations. The Safavids fell to an Afghan invasion, but Ottoman and Mughal political decline corresponded with the rise of the European colonialist enterprise. The encounter with colonialism presented opportunities for Islamic (and more secularizing modes of) political thought. For some, exposure to European ideas of political liberalism led to a search for corresponding ideas in the Islamic tradition. For others, the historically unusual experience of domination by non-Muslims suggested that the core Muslim values and practices that had led to such conspicuous success in the past had fallen into desuetude and thus required reviving. Both approaches negotiated a complex path between local interests and ideas of pan-Islamic liberation and unity, and were also in dialogue with secular ideologies such as socialism and nationalism.

Some postcolonial nation-states, whether traditional monarchies or quasi-republican/parliamentarian, have sought to claim varying degrees of legitimacy in Islamic terms. Constitutions are a conspicuous site of such claims and reveal the complex pressures of religion on modern statehood. The Egyptian constitution of 1971, for example, provides in article 2 (as amended in 1980) that "the principles of Islamic law shall be the primary source of legislation," and the Pakistani constitution proclaims in the very first sentence of its preamble that "sovereignty over the entire universe belongs to Almighty Allah alone." Monarchies, too, are attracted by Islamic constitutionalism. Saudi Arabia's 1992 Basic Law of Governance states in article 1 that Saudi Arabia's official religion is Islam, and that the Qur'an ("God's Book," *kitâb Allâh*) and the Sunna ("Tradition") of his Messenger (Muhammad) are its "constitution" *(dustûr)*. These are aspirational statements, interesting for their combination of theological and nontheological commitments. In general, such constitutional provisions respond to three sets of challenges. One is to appeal to political constituencies that wish to see an expanded role for Islam in the activities of the state. Another is to respond to those critics of a given state who denounce that state as fundamentally un-Islamic. A final challenge is presented by the much more fully realized vision of an Islamic state that Iran represents. Among many interesting provisions, it acknowledges the Imam's role in guiding the state in its pursuit of Islamic ideals in article 2.5. That the combination of rule by theologians and democratic processes is a work in progress is shown by the summer 2009 elections, the results of which led to a substantial period of civil unrest and the appearance of major divisions among Iran's leading clerics. The early, definitive split between religious authority and political authority in Sunnism makes it difficult to imagine such an experiment in clerical rule being undertaken by Sunnis.

PART V

INTERACTIONS

Chapter Twelve

WOMEN AND ISLAM

Homayra Ziad

The Qur'an and Women

The Qur'an is a remarkably egalitarian scripture when it comes to the pivotal moments of creation and judgment, making no spiritual distinction between women and men: both are created from a single soul, and both reap the rewards of God-centered action equally (e.g., Q 3:195; 4:1; 40:39-40). It celebrates the fundamental humanity of women and significantly raises the status of women on the economic, legal, and personal fronts. Widespread misogynist practices, such as female infanticide and the abuse of slave girls for sexual pleasure, are emphatically denounced, and practices such as polygamy, divorce, and concubinage are restricted. But the Qur'an does make gender-based distinctions at the level of social interaction, and by contemporary standards many of its social pronouncements appear nonegalitarian.

Although the Qur'an prescribes a society in which women have the right to independent economic and legal personhood, it speaks the language of a seventh-century tribal society in which social patriarchy is the norm and men are women's legal and economic guardians. The verses containing social pronouncements have been the focal point of most contemporary Muslim and non-Muslim critiques of the Qur'an, as well as the inspiration for Muslim feminist attempts at reinterpreting the text. The most contentious verses in this regard are those traditionally interpreted to suggest that men are "in charge of" women *(qawwâmûn 'ala al-nisâ')*, based on an inherent degree of advantage *(daraja)*. Using the Qur'an itself, several modern scholars have, for example, convincingly argued against the essential nature of this "degree," noting that the Qur'an links this notion to economic advantage, and that with the change in women's earning capacity, this idea should no longer apply.

For the Qur'an, marriage is an institution rooted in God-consciousness and mutual support ("Your [wives] are as a garment for you, and you are as a garment for them" [Q 2:187]). While wives are asked to make themselves sexually available to their husbands, husbands are asked to be conscious of God and their own souls when seeking sexual gratification from their wives. Many scholars see the latter as guarding against the possibility of marital rape. Women's sexuality is to be expressed only within marriage, but sexuality for men can also be expressed through the institution of concubinage (with "those whom your right hands possess"). However, sex with enslaved women against their will is expressly forbidden; men are urged to marry them as concubines instead. Modernist scholars view concubinage as expressed in the Qur'an as they do slavery, namely, a practice not encouraged and severely curtailed, and meant to be phased out over time.

The Qur'an acknowledges the reality of divorce, but encourages reconciliation; it recommends the appointment of family arbiters from both sides. Verses on divorce are adamant about safeguarding the emotional and economic interests of women. While men retain the right of unilateral divorce, women are granted "the selfsame rights and obligations, in keeping with fairness" (Q 2:228), though many exegetes, invoking men's "degree," have viewed men's rights in divorce as paramount. Divorce must involve two stages before being finalized. A premenopausal woman must wait three menstrual periods to ensure that she is not pregnant. During this period, she may remain in her marriage home and must be left in peace. If she is pregnant, it is recommended that the couple reconcile. If divorce proceeds, the husband does not have the right to take back marital gifts or act vindictively. If a divorced woman is pregnant, the husband must financially support her through the term of her pregnancy and nursing.

While the Qur'an acknowledges the biological reality of childbearing for women and the difficulties of carrying, bearing, and nursing, it does not spell out distinct and biologically determined social functions for men and women. Husbands must maintain wives through two full years of nursing, though the couple is also permitted to wean their child with a wet nurse. At the same time, several oft-quoted Prophetic hadiths celebrate the exalted status of the mother, in which the respect accorded mothers far surpasses that accorded fathers.

Women are accepted as legal persons, on a par with men. In cases dealing with economic matters, however, a woman's testimony must be supported by the testimony of another woman, though in accusations of adultery the wife's testimony of innocence trumps her husband's accusation. And in line with the patrilineal economic structure envisaged by the Qur'an, daughters inherit half the amount given to sons, but this stipulation — one that in any case was often circumvented historically by granting daughters gifts that brought their inheritance to a par with their brothers — has been revisited by modernist scholars.

The possibility of polygamy (a man marrying more than one wife, and up to four) is also expressed within an economic context, cautioning male guardians who may be tempted to covet the property of female orphans in their care. In this case, the Qur'an considers it better that they marry up to four of these wards, on condition that each woman is treated equally. The Qur'an warns men to marry only one woman if they fear they cannot adhere to these stringent standards. Women are expected to marry one man, and the dowry *(mahr)* — before Islam, gifted to the bride's male guardian — was now to be granted directly to her. The Qur'an gives men the right to marry Christians and Jews, but its silence on this matter with regard to women has been historically interpreted as implying its impermissibility, though a number of religious leaders in Western Muslim communities have started endorsing marriages between (largely educated and economically self-sufficient) Muslim women and Christian and Jewish men.

The verse that ostensibly permits husbands to strike their wives as a last resort for "disobedience" (4:34) has been the subject of much controversy. This passage caused much discomfort to medieval commentators, who translated the word as "strike" but softened the implications by invoking a hadith stating that the Prophet Muhammad never struck women and severely chastised other men for doing so. Contemporary scholars have approached this verse in a variety of ways, offering a range of nonviolent interpretations of the meaning, from "not having sex with" to "staying apart from."

The Qur'an directly addresses women as participants in the process of revelation, referring to the women who pledged allegiance to Muhammad independently of their male relatives. Women in early Islam played a significant role in the early Muslim community: they appear to have had relatively free access to the Prophet, were crucial in making his mission a success, and believed that the revelation would respond to them in times of need. When Khawla came to the Prophet to protest an unjust divorce —

her husband had abandoned her, saying, "you are to me like the back of my mother" — the Qur'an specifically prohibited this form of divorce in a sura named for Khawla (*al-Mujâdila,* "The Disputant").

The very first convert to the new religion was a woman, Muhammad's first wife, Khadîja, with whom he remained in a monogamous twenty-five-year relationship until her death. When they first met, she was his employer, twice widowed and some fifteen years his senior. She became his most trusted adviser. In Medina, and after Khadîja's death, Muhammad married several women. Most of these marriages were either political alliances or means of providing support to war widows; others, however, like the marriage to Zaynab, were based on attraction. All the women involved, except for 'Â'isha, were divorcees or widows, and all, in particular 'Â'isha and Umm-Salama, were central to the creation of the hadith corpus, the narrative reports of what the Prophet did, said, or tacitly approved. Women's voices are clearly heard in this literature, often questioning or raised in dissent.

After Muhammad's death, his wives were granted exemplary status ("Mothers of the Believers"). While forbidden to remarry, they nevertheless played key, and at times controversial, political and scholarly roles within the early community. Khadîja, 'Â'isha, and Fâtima (Khadîja and Muhammad's daughter) all became sources of emulation early in the development of the post-Prophetic Muslim community, and were linked with specific pious Qur'anic figures (most often Mary). This resulted in a special literature, which emphasizes particular aspects of the lives of these three women in order to create a portrait of an ideal woman. Additionally, Fâtima gained a devotional status in Shi'ite communal identity that parallels that of the Virgin Mary in Catholicism. Indeed, Mary, the mother of Jesus, is one of several key female figures in the Qur'an. The tender Qur'anic treatment of Mary (an entire sura, "Maryam," is devoted to her) led early theologians to debate seriously the possibility of Mary being a prophet. Other prominent women in the Qur'an include the adoptive mother of Moses and the Queen of Sheba.

Women and Exegesis

Qur'anic injunctions concerning women were drastically reenvisioned by classical Muslim scholarship into a system in which women were placed at a severe social and spiritual disadvantage. The openness and pluralism of Sunni traditionalism, otherwise a great strength in accommodating the message of the Qur'an to diverse cultural settings, in fact worked against Muslim women, as cultural traditions of misogyny found their way into the tradition. The soon-to-be canonical texts of the tradition were authored by male scholars who were products of these cultures and comfortable with nonegalitarian gender norms. The ninth-century jurist al-Shâfiʿî (d. 820) established the scholarly consensus *(ijmâʿ)* of previous generations of scholars as one among several means for resolving complex jurisprudential issues in which the Qur'an and Hadith were either in seeming conflict or not explicit, and made the interpretations of such scholars into an authoritative body of opinion through which the Qur'an and Hadith could be read. Early interpretive activity thus became viewed in many cases as authoritative statements of the Qur'an's legal import. In addition, al-Shâfiʿî's development of hermeneutical techniques encouraged legal interpretation of the Qur'an through the lens of hadith texts, with the result that Hadith could be used to make substantive and far-reaching modifications to Qur'anic legislation.

Similarly, classical Qur'anic exegetes (sometimes Christian and Jewish converts) tended to read the Qur'anic parables on women through the prism of biblical exegesis, expressing fear of women's sexuality and inclination toward evil. Thus, the story of Joseph and the wife of the Egyptian nobleman is read as a commentary on women's inherent cunning and violent sexual desire. Classical and medieval exegetes blame Eve for the Fall, but in the Qur'an it is both Adam and "his spouse" who disobey God. By contrast, modern commentators have tended to reverse this trend, reading passages on women for their ethical content and in light of changing gender norms. Modernists like Muhammad ʿAbduh (d. 1905) and fundamentalists like Sayyid Qutb (d. 1966) both emphasize the spiritual equality and individual moral responsibility of men and women; for Qutb, women are equal to men as warriors in the path of God. Interestingly, conservative commentators, while insisting on male and female spiritual equality, continue to employ biblical conceptions of Adam and Eve to point out psychological differences between men and women, and uphold norms of gender segregation and women's confinement to child rearing and the home.

Women and Hadith

We find the greatest antifemale sentiment in the hadiths, which characterize women as temptresses, unclean, unfaithful, and morally deficient.

However, the most misogynist hadiths were later (eleventh-century) additions to the ninth- and tenth-century canonical compilations. Out of numerous hadiths with antifemale content, only six are recognized by scholarly consensus as authenticated, and yet these hadiths are pervasive in scholarly discourses relating to women. Meanwhile, duly authenticated hadiths *(sahîh)* that affirm women's humanity and the foundation of marriage as justice and love, that exalt mothers over fathers, that acknowledge women's status as evidence givers, and that recognize women's right to knowledge, to mixed-gender public space (both religious and secular), and to choice of dress have all been largely ignored.

Women and Activity in the Public Space

Because the law upheld Qur'anic support for female inheritance and independent ownership of wealth, women were able to engage in economic activity. According to court records from all over the Muslim empire, women of the middle classes owned property and were active in business, while wealthy women also took part in trade. During the medieval period, it was very common for wealthy women to endow and patronize charities, spiritual retreats, and mosques. Mamlûk women endowed educational establishments *(madrasas)* and held supervisory roles in administration, management of assets, and appointing of faculty and staff. Women associated with the Indian Mughal court made significant contributions to the cultural life of the empire, patronizing the arts, innovating perfumes, designing gardens and textile patterns, and influencing the direction of miniature art. Sewing, embroidery, and other forms of textile production provided income for women of modest means; occupations open to less privileged women included servant, midwife, food seller, bath attendant, baker, peddler, professional mourner, singer, and prostitute. In cases of injustice, women did not hesitate to take legal action. Many women apparently represented themselves in court, and their testimony held equal weight to that of men.

The domain of religious scholarship was defined by men, but women appear surprisingly often in biographical dictionaries of religious professionals. The women who gained access to this domain usually grew up in middle-class or elite scholarly families, and their educational trajectory was launched and encouraged by male relatives. They were recognized as muftis (legal experts); they studied, recited, and copied the Qur'an; and they received certificates from male scholars that allowed them to teach. Many revered scholars, such as Ibn-Hajar (d. 1448), are reported to have had female teachers. Women also played a significant role in the normative arena of hadith transmission, and were regularly cited in the chains of transmission of major Sunni compilations. Importantly, female hadith scholars dealt directly with men in both public and private educational spaces, including mosques, and their students included both men and women, in mixed-gender gatherings.

Women were also active participants in public ritual life. One woman, Umm-Waraqa, was appointed prayer leader for her household *(dâr)* by Muhammad. In fact, contemporary debates over whether women can lead public mixed-gender prayers stem from divergent understandings of the term *dâr* in this hadith (as referring to a household, or a larger area).

Women and Sufism

Sufi literary and biographical works often depict women who surpass their male counterparts in pursuits of mind and spirit. Râbi'a of Basra, for example, is considered one of the pioneers of Sufi thought, articulating the vocabulary of love as a means of approach to the divine. She is presented as a revered critic of male spiritual arrogance; thus, a woman's subversive words and actions are an integral part of the founding discourse of Sufism. An eleventh-century biographical work by al-Sulamî reveals that many women carved out roles as devotees, spiritual teachers, and social critics that transcended sociocultural gender norms and earned the respect of male counterparts. The great Sufi Ibn-'Arabî (d. 1240) credited much of his learning to two female teachers. Fittingly, rather than as a symbol of female cunning, the figure of the Egyptian nobleman's wife entranced by Joseph is seen in Sufi literature as symbolic of perfect absorption in the divine. Sufi works were not immune to misogyny, however. At times, female physical processes like menstruation were portrayed as a handicap on the spiritual path, and women themselves as obstacles to a man's spiritual life. Women, especially those who were part of a Sufi master's *(shaykh)* family, often performed tasks, duties, and ritual observances, but institutionally, Sufi women were rarely formally designated *shaykha*, even if a female disciple held the greatest spiritual potential. Many Sufi orders do, however, have separate women's groups with female spiritual leadership.

Women's religiosity is thus expressed less in mosques and more at the shrines of Sufi saints (both men and women), who continue to command great popular appeal and are seen to possess miraculous powers even in death. Because the Sufi tradition did not see social class and education as barriers to spiritual enlightenment, women have found a safe ritual space at shrines, and many saints are said to respond to uniquely female problems, like infertility. In some areas, such as parts of Morocco and South Asia, women form the majority of visitors to Sufi shrines. In many countries, the rituals associated with the festivals that accompany the death anniversaries of saints *('urs, mawlid)*, like the annual pilgrimage to the Ka'ba, are conducted in nonsegregated spaces. But the mixing of genders and the existence of ecstatic devotional practices in which women can take part have made shrine visitation a hot-button issue for conservative reformers, who seek to eradicate this practice.

Women and Colonialism

While colonial reform of personal status laws played a part in dismantling premodern structures for the control and exclusion of women, the new law codes incorporated Victorian ideals of marriage and an essentialized, biologically determined role for each sex. At the same time, they incorporated narrow readings of a limited set of religious texts declared to be scripturally authoritative. Women also lost ground in the area of education. For instance, while the Egyptian ruler Khedive Ismâ'îl (ruled 1863-1879) tried to meet the growing demand for men and women's education, the 1882 British colonial occupation of Egypt discouraged and curbed this demand. Female students were the most severely affected, and by the period of the First World War (1914-1918) the number of girls attending government schools in Egypt had actually fallen to below 1890 levels. It was on the level of discourse that women lost the greatest ground under colonial rule, as issues concerning women, culture, and nationalism became inextricably bound together, and remain so today. Images of the oppressed Muslim woman have been critical to the colonial construction of a culturally inferior Muslim "other," and colonial officials and scholars duly appropriated the discourse of feminism to justify European domination. Women's issues became the touchstone for reform. Rather than being invited to engage constructively with their own cultures, Muslim women were instead urged to adopt an entirely new, ostensibly superior, European, Christian culture. In this discourse, the very visible institution of the head covering/veil *(hijâb)* came to be regarded as symbolic of women's oppression. That the language of feminism was used mostly as a rhetorical tool is evidenced by the fact that many prominent colonial administrators were actually opposing women's emancipation in their own countries. Lord Cromer, the British consul general in Egypt, was a strong supporter of the unveiling of Egyptian women, but at the same time a founding member of the Men's League for Opposing Women's Suffrage in England.

Colonial discourse on the veil was also adopted by Muslim reformers. Muhammad Qâsim Amîn's 1899 book *The Liberation of Woman* has long been regarded as revolutionary for its calls for reforms of polygamy and divorce laws, granting women primary education and abolishing the veil. But Amîn, like his contemporary Ashraf Ali Thânwî (d. 1943), and like al-Tahtâwî (d. 1873) and 'Abduh before them, saw women as both the source of all social ills and the bearers of societal virtue, and thus in need of being saved from themselves by men. Stripping women of the veil was Amîn's solution, but one that simply replicated the colonialist perspective. Henceforth, women and culture in Muslim reformist discourse (whether secular or religious) would be permanently linked, and the veil would become a key signifier within this discourse. Opposition to colonialism would also appropriate the vocabulary of colonial discourse, whereby the veil would come to represent the dignity of indigenous culture. The debate over whether veiling is explicitly mandated in the Qur'an (24:31-32) continues unabated, as does the debate over whether gender segregation is prescribed in the context of all women or only the Prophet's wives, who were asked to remain in their homes, for they "are not like other women" (Q 33:32).

Women, the Modern State, and Political Islam

Fearing a conservative backlash, the state in most Muslim-majority countries has been reluctant to interfere with the personal status laws that were crystallized under colonial regimes. Largely based on narrow and unstructured interpretations of Islamic jurisprudence, these laws had become associated by Muslim men with the core of Muslim identity under colonialism. However, economic pressures that necessitated women's engagement in the labor market, as well as political pressure from prominent women's groups, led to significant reforms in personal status law during the twentieth century. Some countries abolished polygamy, while others made it exceedingly difficult to practice. Women also made other significant gains in the realms of marriage, divorce, and child custody, although it is not a little ironic that many of these same rights were actually granted women in the Qur'an but had never been put into practice.

Throughout the twentieth century, however, the state has also used personal status laws to achieve its own interests. On the one hand, the harnessing of productive female workers and voters through the reform of personal status was essential for the economic and political success of the state. On the other hand, conservative ideologues, who continue to connect the dots between women's public role, modernization, Westernization, imperialism, and the fall of Islamic civilization, and who garner considerable public support, still need to be appeased. This usually takes place through periodic imposition of modesty codes on women, and changes in marriage and divorce laws that are detrimental to women, exemplified by measures adopted in Iran immediately after the revolution and in Pakistan under the military dictator Zia-ul-Haq (d. 1988). In both cases, women became tools in games of political and patriarchal dominance.

Women have become increasingly involved in the institutions of political Islam, through groups such as Hezbollah, the Muslim Brotherhood, and Jamaat-i-Islami, and are creating new paradigms for women's activism that reject Western secular feminism. Unlike secular reform movements, which remain largely urban and elite, Islamist movements have broad grassroots appeal that transcends social class boundaries and have successfully adopted the instruments of party politics (campaigning, mobilizing). Women have been essential to the success of these movements — some, like Maryam Jameelah (Jamaat-i-Islami) and Zaynab al-Ghâzalî (Muslim Brotherhood), have served as important spokespersons — and are now asking for more significant political leadership roles.

Women as Political Leaders

Despite the widespread acceptance of a hadith ostensibly decrying female leadership, and the definition of politics as an exclusively male domain, many Muslim women have held significant political leadership roles, some independently and some jointly with their husbands, such as Khayzurân, who governed the Abbasid empire under three caliphs in the eighth century. Others include two Yemeni queens; a Berber queen; a Fâtimid queen of Egypt in the eleventh century; two thirteenth-century Mamlûk queens, in Cairo and Delhi; a dynasty of Mongol queens in the thirteenth century;

a fifteenth-century queen in Islamic Spain; four seventeenth-century queens of Indonesia; and five Begums who ruled the princely state of Bhopal in the nineteenth and twentieth centuries.

In the postcolonial era, women have assumed the highest roles of political leadership in Muslim countries, though as always it is rare for women to achieve political prominence without family patronage. Women have become prime ministers and presidents of some of the most populous Muslim countries: Benazir Bhutto in Pakistan (1988-1990, 1993-1996), Tansu Ciller in Turkey (1993-1996), Khaleda Zia (1991-1996, 2001-2006) and Sheikh Hasina in Bangladesh (1996-2001, and currently), and Megawati Sukarnoputri (2001-2004) in Indonesia. The impact of their position on the rights of women in their respective nations has not been great, but women are slowly finding their way into national assemblies and parliaments in majority Muslim countries, helped by nongovernmental women's rights groups as well as state quotas.

Chapter Thirteen

ISLAM AND JUDAISM

Mark S. Wagner

For most people who contemplate the relationship between Islam and Judaism, object lessons in the deep-seated "ancient hatreds" that threaten world stability in the post–Cold War world spring immediately to mind. Among Jews, the claim to the land of Israel commands a near total consensus, while opposition to this claim has become a de facto tenet of world Islam. Viewed in this light, the enmity between Muslims and Jews is regarded as virtually a law of nature. Many are shocked, therefore, to learn that, historically, the moments of contact between Islam and Judaism show variety, complexity, intellectual depth, and even beauty. Jewish and Muslim intellectuals have consistently grappled with the deeply rooted and varied interconnectedness of these religions ever since the rise of Islam.

Judaism, both its scriptural traditions and praxis, played an important role in the formation of Islam, and for centuries most Jews in the world lived in Muslim polities and spoke Muslim languages. Among them, Islam played a crucial role in shaping Jewish law, ritual, intellectual life, and culture, in short, those interconnected activities that together constitute Judaism as it is known today. Before the modern period, Muslims and Jews did not interact as equals but rather as ruler and minority. Thus Jewish sources demonstrate Islam's impact on Judaism far more consistently than the reverse.

In the vein of the Prophet Muhammad's "Constitution of Medina" (see "Islamic Government," chapter 11), the "Pact of 'Umar" (a document attributed either to the third caliph, 'Umar, or to a later caliph of the same name) laid out regulations that, while not enforced consistently, played a large part in defining the parameters of Muslim-Jewish interaction in the Islamic world. These regulations, as well as the collection of a mandatory tax (the *jizya*), dramatized in the public sphere the subservient status of the non-Muslims who lived at the indulgence of the Islamic state — Islamic law reckoned Jews, along with the far more numerous Christians (and later also Hindus), to be "people of the pact [of protection]" *(dhimmîs)*. Despite this, Jews and Judaism seem to have occupied more than their fair share of the Muslim imagination. The ninth-century Muslim writer al-Jâhiz remarked that Muslims disliked Jews more than they disliked Christians because Jews and Muslims resemble one another and people dislike those who are similar more than those who are different. Tales of wicked Jews who practice black magic that appear in the *Thousand and One Nights* and a chapter about "the fraudulence of Jewish men of learning" in a thirteenth-century manual of con jobs attest to some widespread stereotypes of Jews among Muslims.

Scholars of the relationship between Islam and Judaism have generated a number of compelling metaphors for Islam and Judaism's interdependence, speaking of "creative symbiosis"; "the Judeo-Islamic tradition"; or "full circles" through which Jewish ideas enter Islam, become Islamicized, then reenter Judaism, though these images occasionally obscure the asymmetry of the relationship. The image of ecumenical gates between Judaism and Islam, around which some adventurous Jews and Muslims congregated and beyond which some Jews strayed, helps isolate some of the main areas of interaction between Islam and Judaism. These include scripture, law, theology, philosophy and the sciences, mysticism, literary culture, music, and modern scholarship. Arabic sources on the birth of Islam depict a steadily deteriorating relationship between the Prophet Muhammad and the fledgling Muslim *umma* on one side and the well-established Jewish communities of the Arabian Peninsula on the other. With the exception of the episode of the massacre of the Jewish Qurayza tribe — the historicity of which some scholars have called into question — the critical scrutiny brought to bear on Arabic sources on earliest Islam has skirted the topic of the Jews of that period. It is clear that from at least the eighth century Muslims have seen their religion as moving from an initial intimacy with Judaism and reliance on its prophetology, sacred history, and rituals, to mature independence, a change embodied in a story of how Muhammad shifted the direction of prayer *(qibla)* from Jerusalem to Mecca.

Scripture

The preponderance in the Qur'an of stories and characters deriving from the Hebrew Bible and its rabbinic amplifications (in Hebrew, *midrash*) has attracted enormous interest among scholars. The story of the "women of the city" who, beholding Joseph's beauty, cut their hands rather than pieces of fruit, appears in the Qur'an and in *Tanhuma-Yelamdenu,* a collection of *midrashim* that was probably compiled around the rise of Islam. This example illustrates one of the thorniest problems for scholars: Given the difficulty of dating the extant collections of rabbinic *midrash,* is rabbinic material in the Qur'an and in Muslim exegesis *(tafsîr)* in fact rabbinic, or did Qur'anic retellings of biblical stories find their way into these most Jewish of works?

For Muslim scholars in the traditional mold, the divine, revelatory origin of the Qur'anic text renders moot historical questions of cultural influence. Nevertheless, objections to outlandish "Israelite tales" *(Isrâ'îliyyât)* interspersed within the corpus of Muslim exegetical traditions were voiced from the tenth century onward. Many Muslims who were most keen on weeding out *Isrâ'îliyyât,* such as Ibn-Kathîr (d. 1373), or Sayyid Qutb (d. 1966) in the twentieth century, themselves used Jewish material in interpreting the Qur'an. For premodern Muslim scholarship, identifying *Isrâ'îliyyât* served as a way to explain the dissonance between biblical and midrashic accounts of the prophets' transgressions and the Islamic doctrine of prophetic sinlessness *('isma).*

One figure to whom many such Israelite tales are attributed is Ka'b-al-Ahbâr (d. 652), a Jewish convert to Islam. Arabic sources say he identified the location of the ancient Jerusalem temple for an early caliph, who proceeded to build the Dome of the Rock over that spot. Jewish amulets and other folk art depicted this Islamic monument, along with the adjacent al-Aqsâ Mosque, (anachronistically) to represent the temple. It would not have been unusual for a Jewish family in eastern Europe to mark the wall facing Jerusalem with a plaque containing a representation of these Muslim monuments.

Muslims adopted the theme, already present in late antique Judaism and early Christianity, of the stiff-necked and disobedient Jew who rejects the prophets (in the episode of the golden calf, for example). The Muslim idea that Jews (and Christians) had deliberately tampered with God's word, a doctrine called *tahrîf,* was novel, but allowed for two contradictory stances toward the Hebrew Bible: (1) Jews excised references to Muhammad's mission from the Hebrew Bible but some may have escaped these editorial efforts; (2) the Hebrew Bible is a thoroughly besmirched text and is thus unworthy of consideration as scripture. Although the second position dominated Muslim intellectual life, numerous Muslim authors discussed the Hebrew Bible. Most consulted Jews about its contents, but two writers, Ibn-Hazm (d. 1064) and al-Biqâ'î (d. 1480), wrote highly original analyses likely based upon translations of the Hebrew Bible into Arabic. And the pervasiveness of the Qur'an in Islamic culture was such that, when Se'adya Gaon (d. 942) translated the Hebrew Bible into Arabic, he called the "red heifer" of Numbers 19:2 a "yellow cow" *(baqara safrâ')* in conscious or unconscious imitation of Q 2:69, though in fact Jews seldom made direct reference to the Qur'an because they were forbidden by the Pact of 'Umar from studying it.

Law and Theology

Islam in its Sunni (see "Sunnis, Sunnism," chapter 9) and Shi'ite (see "Shi'ites, Shi'ism," chapter 8) iterations emerged out of the vibrant intellectual life of the new city of Baghdad, founded in 762. The venerable rabbinic academies of Sura and Pumbeditha (modern-day Fallujah) relocated to Baghdad soon after the city's founding, setting the stage for intense intellectual contacts between Muslims and Jews at the highest institutional levels. Islam and Judaism share a virtually identical mind-set regarding the centrality of law. Given that the emergence of Islamic legal theory was roughly coterminous with the elaboration of Jewish law by the Geonim, the spiritual leaders of Jewry, the relationship between Jewish law and Islamic law remains a rich topic of inquiry.

Se'adya Gaon, a pivotal figure in Judaism, composed Hebrew poetry, wrote extensive works on law and polemic, made the first translation of the Hebrew Bible into Arabic, and wrote a work of Jewish systematic theology, *The Book of Beliefs and Opinions,* that led to his description by a twelfth-century Jewish writer of Muslim Spain, Abraham Ibn-Ezra (d. 1167), as "first and foremost among the rationalistic theologians." Se'adya was thus the first Jewish "Mu'tazilî" (see "Islamic Philosophy," chapter 6). Mu'tazilite thought, particularly in its criticism of authoritative traditions and discomfort with anthropomorphism, made a great impression upon several Geonim. A movement called Karaism (which accepts the Hebrew Bible but rejects rabbinic Judaism and the Mishnah and the Talmud as binding) took the Muʿtazilî criticism of tradition a step further than the Geonim by rejecting the authority of rabbinic sources altogether. Rabbinic authorities therefore deemed Karaism heretical, although practically speaking the two groups often coexisted. The Muʿtazilî school valued interconfessional disputation with Jews, among others. One tenth-century Muslim visitor to Baghdad attended a theological discussion organized by Muʿtazilî and was scandalized by the participants, a rogues' gallery of Muslims of all stripes, atheists, and non-Muslims, as well as by the rules of the discussion, which precluded arguments rooted in scripture. A number of Jewish intellectuals converted to Islam as a result of Muʿtazilî disputations. Since Muʿtazilism was later deemed heterodox and largely stamped out in Islam, reconstructing the history and doctrine of this chapter in Islamic thought relies to a great extent on (Karaite) Jewish sources.

The practice of insulting the Prophet *(sabb al-rasûl)* constituted a capital crime for both Muslims and non-Muslims, so criticisms of the Prophet Muhammad could be dangerous and were generally avoided. Some Jews did criticize the Qur'an's status as scripture. In tenth-century Iraq, rabbinic and Karaite writers argued against the Muslim doctrine that the Torah had been abrogated by the revelation of the Qur'an. If God sends new dispensations at certain intervals known only to him, Seʿadya argued, has he not changed? Moreover, what grounds existed to claim that the Qur'an would not suffer the same fate? The Karaite Yûsuf al-Basîr (d. 1040) tackled the doctrine of the inimitability of the Qur'an *(iʿjâz)* by arguing that would-be prophets other than Muhammad imitated it, questioning the good faith of the Qur'an's redactors, and suggesting that many of those Arabs who could have imitated the Qur'an refrained from doing so because they were intimidated by Muslim political power. In twelfth-century Spain, Moses Ibn-Ezra made similar arguments, calling attention to attempts by Muslim writers to imitate the Qur'an, whose success or lack thereof was a matter of taste. Ibn-Kammûna (d. 1284), a Jewish philosopher of the Mongol period, wrote an audacious work in which he cast doubt on the motives of converts to Islam. According to one Arab historian, he was as a result forced to flee Baghdad and go into hiding. In addition to these relatively abstract debates, the conspiracy theory that a renegade Jewish scholar forged the Qur'an, as well as various unkind characterizations of Muhammad, made the rounds among Jews behind closed doors.

Philosophy and Science

Philosophy, specifically an admixture of Aristotelianism and Neoplatonism, constituted another ecumenical gate through which Muslims and Jews interacted. This was not surprising in that it was explicitly nonreligious in orientation. When translating Muslim works into Hebrew, Jewish philosophers simply replaced Qur'anic verses with comparable quotations from the Hebrew Scriptures and identified prophetic hadiths as heretofore lost rabbinic sayings. Moses ben Maimon (Maimonides, d. 1204) wrote authoritative works of Jewish law and an esoteric, Aristotelian reading of the Hebrew Bible entitled *The Guide of the Perplexed*. For centuries Jews have asked if the Maimonides of orthodox Judaism can be squared with Maimonides the philosopher. His views on Islam were similarly complex, as he argued in one place that Muhammad's mission was a boon to monotheism and elsewhere that "never did a nation degrade, debase, and hate us as much as [the Arabs]."

Medicine brought some Jews in close contact with power. A Muslim official brought about a dozen Jewish physicians into the Ayyûbid court in Egypt, including Maimonides, who served as court physician to Saladin in Cairo. Among Maimonides' medical works are treatises on the effects of poison, sex, and hemorrhoids — topics of perennial interest to powerful aging men. In the sixteenth century, Jewish physicians served the Ottoman sultans in several capacities. Solomon ben Nathan Ashkenazi (d. 1602), an Italian Jew who studied medicine in Padua, served as the principal adviser to Selim II and Murad III. In addition to his medical practice, he worked as a high-level diplomat and business tycoon. One Jewish physician, Sa'd-al-dawla, rose to become second-in-command to the Mongol Ilkhân Arghûn. A Muslim chronicler attributed his precipitous fall from grace (and subsequent attacks on Jewish communities) to having stretched out his legs impudently during a game of backgammon with the sovereign. In Granada in the Muslim West, the Jewish vizier and poet Shmuel ha-Nagid (d. 1056) courted similar controversy.

Yet even in science, the most ecumenical of pursuits, some Muslim teachers were loath to admit non-Muslim pupils to their study circles. Abû-al-Barakât al-Baghdâdî (d. ca. 1164) became a Muslim in order to study with a famous physician of Baghdad; reportedly, so did Isaac Ibn-Ezra (flourished in the twelfth century), the son of Abraham Ibn-Ezra (d. ca. 1167), the great Spanish biblical exegete, philosopher, and astronomer. Ismâ'îlî Shi'ite Muslims arranged interreligious disputations, mainly for the purposes of conversion. Even so, the curious blend of Islamic prophetology and Neoplatonism pioneered by Ismâ'îlî thinkers made a strong impact upon a number of Jewish intellectuals. In his *Garden of Intellects,* the Yemenite Jew Netanael al-Fayyûmî (flourished in the twelfth century) distinguishes himself in this regard for his application of the parochially Shi'ite concept of the imamate to Judaism.

Mysticism

The mystical side of Islam (see "Sufism," chapter 7) drew in Jews of all social classes with its stress on interior experience over intellectual pursuits (such as theology and law) and its promise of intimacy with the divine. The thirteenth-century mystic Ibn-'Arabî spoke to the ecumenical character of membership in a Sufi circle when he described his heart as "a monastery for Christian monks, and a temple for idols, and the pilgrim's Ka'ba, and the tablets of the Torah and the book of the Qur'an." Maimonides' son, Abraham, wrote that Sufis preserved an essential Judaism that contemporary Jews had lost. When he tried to introduce prostration into the synagogue service, irate congregants complained to the sultan that he was trying to Islamicize Judaism. The sultan sided with them, but the activities of Maimonides' descendants ensured the survival of Jewish Sufism in Egypt for centuries. The Cairo Genizah, a massive trove of documents from a synagogue in Cairo crucial for reconstructing the life of ordinary people in the medieval Middle East, includes a letter from a woman to the leader of the Jewish community in Egypt complaining that her husband has sold their property and joined a Sufi commune.

The Hebrew religious poetry of the Spanish rabbi Judah Halevi is marked by such Sufi themes as dream visions and includes at least one direct translation of an Arabic Sufi poem. His classic statement of Jewish chosenness, *The Kuzari,* bears the imprint of Sufi doctrines too. Another Spanish Jew, Bahya ben Pakuda, drew from Sufi traditions to write his pietistic manual, widely known as *The Duties of the Heart.* Hasidic Jews in eighteenth-century Europe sought inspiration in Bahya's book (in Hebrew translation) for their grassroots mysticism. Thus, through Bahya, the famous hadith attributed to Muhammad, "You have returned from the lesser struggle *(jihâd),* now prepare for the greater struggle *(jihâd)* [with your passions]," became a story by Rabbi Jacob Joseph of Polonnoye in Ukraine. From there it has become standard fare for Yom Kippur homilies in liberal synagogues.

Iranian Jewish literature reflects the Persianate world's saturation with Islamic mysticism. Epics written in Judeo-Persian recast biblical accounts in the mold of heroic sagas of ancient Persian kings such as Ferdowsi's *Shâh-nameh*. In his *Fath-nâmeh (Epic of the Conquests)*, 'Imrânî (late fifteenth century) enlivens the arid biblical account of the Israelite conquests by punctuating it with Sufi trances. He describes the priests who sounded the ram's horn at the walls of Jericho as being "absorbed in union with God, uttering 'there is no God but God,' the leaders in a state of ecstasy."

Literature and the Arts

Arabic poems by and about Jews predate Islam; the Jewish poet al-Samaw'al is proverbial for his fidelity. Another Jewish poet, Ka'b-ibn-al-Ashrâf, is remembered for casting aspersions on Muhammad. Jews in Islamic Spain wrote poetry in Arabic, but they also engineered an exciting new literary form by applying the aesthetic conventions of Arabic poetry to Hebrew poetry. Some justified this by arguing that the Arabs had learned eloquence (along with religion) from the Jews. One Hebrew writer in Spain said of an Arabic classic, the *Assemblies (Maqâmât)* of al-Harîrî, "Demand of its every trope, How came you here to stand? And the latter will reply, I was stolen away out of the Hebrews' land" — these are in fact Joseph's words to Pharaoh's chief cupbearer. A Moroccan Jew, Dunash ibn-Labrat (d. 990), devised a way of applying Arabic prosody to Hebrew. Indeed, Hebrew poets adopted the full range of classical Arabic poetry's conventional imagery and rhetorical devices. The most consciously Arabizing of them, Moses Ibn-Ezra, wrote a treatise on "the best path in the composition of Hebrew poetry according to Arabic rules." Because the text of the Hebrew Bible provided their raw material, Hebrew poets made scriptural quotation the cornerstone of their poetics.

In many areas of the Middle East, notably the Levant, North Africa, Yemen, and Iraq, Jews paid close attention to the latest styles in the music and song of their Muslim neighbors. In sixteenth-century Syria, Israel Najarah cleverly lifted the melodies and wording of Ottoman Turkish songs to produce kabbalistic Hebrew poetry. In Morocco in the same century Jews began writing "embroidered" *(matrûz)* poetry, a bilingual genre consisting of Hebrew liturgical poetry interwoven with Muslim (Arabic) songs. Rabbi Shmuel Albaz (d. 1844) and Rabbi David Bouzaglo (d. 1975) left behind corpora of such poems. In seventeenth-century Yemen, Rabbi

Salîm al-Shabazi (d. ca. 1680) appropriated the local vernacular poetry, creating a new form of kabbalistic bilingual (Hebrew-Arabic) poems. This style persisted for centuries. The common denominator in these musical-poetic experiments may have been the new kabbalistic practice of super-erogatory prayers in the middle of the night *(ashmurot ha-boqer)*. At that hour the only audible sounds may have been the music of Muslim revelers, which was incorporated into the ritual.

Jews became prominent in the musical world of the modern Middle East and central Asia. In the early twentieth century humorous songs in Arabic by Jews set to Muslim melodies and recorded for the gramophone became hits in Tunisia. Jews in North Africa defied rabbinic opposition to lyrical Muslim songs by embracing that genre. Two modern Jewish singers, Sâmî al-Maghribî and Zohra al-Fassiyah, were especially popular in Morocco. In Iraq, Jews were the musicians par excellence. When they left Iraq the music industry was left reeling. The cobbler and singer Leviche Babakhanov (d. 1926), enlisted by the emir of Bukhara as his court musician, became a recording sensation in the early twentieth century. Jewish writers in central Asia composed socialist novels and poems in Tajik in the same period. In Egypt, Leila Murâd (d. 1995), the daughter of a cantor, was for a time the most recognized film actress and the "Singer of the Revolution." Though she converted to Islam, she was accused of spying for Israel and lived out her later years in bitter seclusion.

Scholars of Islamic Civilization

Scholarship constituted a last ecumenical gate for Jewish-Muslim interaction. While European Jewish scholars helped shape the contours of modern Arabic and Islamic studies, the ideological currents inside and outside academia in the twentieth and early twenty-first centuries limited them in various ways. Ignaz Goldziher (d. 1921), who pioneered the critical approach to Islamic sources, worked for thirty years as the secretary to a Jewish congregation in Budapest. His Jewishness precluded him from an academic position in a Hungarian university and his Hungarian nationalism kept him from taking a job abroad. By day, the ophthalmologist Max Meyerhof (d. 1945) ran a busy eye clinic in Cairo. At night, by lamplight, he worked on medieval Arabic and Jewish medicine. Once a German patriot who served as a field medic in World War I, Meyerhof renounced his German citizenship with the rise of the Nazi Party and became an Egyptian in 1936.

The European Jewish Orientalists who founded Arabic and Islamic studies at the Hebrew University of Jerusalem conceived of the relationship between Islam and Judaism as the center of the discipline. It remains so in Israeli universities. Yet this intense scholarly interest in the medieval Islamic past, along with the dovish politics of most of these scholars, did not solve the territorial (and, increasingly, religious) conflict between Arabs and Jews. The tendency in contemporary Islamic studies to regard Islam as *sui generis* has diminished Jewish-Muslim interaction in scholarship. In the words of Franz Rosenthal (d. 2003), a notable scholar of Islam and Judeo-Islamica, "cross-cultural and cross-religious relations [are now] read out of existence." But the study of Judeo-Islamic cultures, especially Genizah studies, has received new life through the opening of the Firkovitch collection in St. Petersburg in the early 1990s and sizable private investments. Judeo-Islamic studies flourish as well within academic Jewish studies, in Israeli departments of Arabic and Islamic studies, and in Spain, which is eager to rediscover itself as the bridge between Europe and the Middle East.

Chapter Fourteen

ISLAM AND CHRISTIANITY

Paul Löffler and Mark N. Swanson

Context and Historical Sketch

As the twentieth century drew to its close, many Christians sensed both the urgency and the promise of new developments in the 1,400-year-old history of Christian-Muslim relations. Dramatic gestures such as the visits of Pope John Paul II to Muslim leaders throughout the world communicated the widely felt sense that new Christian attitudes toward Islam were developing and that new conversation and cooperation between Christian and Muslim theologians and institutions were possible. Interest in Islam has increased by leaps and bounds in Europe and North America, due in part to the increasing presence of Muslim guest workers, immigrants (including refugees), and converts. Even in places where Muslims had long been seen as exotic outsiders, Christians began to encounter Muslims in their neighborhoods, in their workplaces, and — through marriage — in their own families.

Christian churches have turned their attention to Islam at denominational and ecumenical levels, and specialized institutes for the study of Christian-Muslim relations have flourished, for example, at the University of Birmingham in the United Kingdom, Hartford Seminary and Georgetown University in the United States, and the Pontificio Istituto di Studi Arabi e d'Islamistica in Rome, Italy. Such interest is by no means limited to the West: some of the most moving testimonies of the possibilities for Christian-Muslim understanding and common work come from the churches of the non-Western world and from institutions such as the

Christian Study Centre in Rawalpindi (Pakistan), the Henry Martyn Institute in Hyderabad (India), and the Program for Christian-Muslim Relations in Africa (formerly the Islam in Africa Project).

The sense of urgency in these new developments in Christian-Muslim relations can be understood only against the background of a long history of hostility and estrangement. Even at the end of the twentieth century, violence involving Christian and Muslim communities continued to be all too common in many parts of the world, including the Sudan, Nigeria, the Balkan states, and parts of Indonesia. While each case is complex and resists classification merely as a religious conflict, each adds its own sad load to the burden of history that continues to weigh down individuals and communities seeking harmonious relations between Christians and Muslims.

Competition between the two faiths was present from the very beginning. Within a decade of the death in 632 of Muhammad, the Prophet of Islam, Muslim armies had conquered a huge part of the ancient Christian heartland, including Palestine, Syria, and Egypt. For centuries, Islam and Christianity were the faiths of competing, expansionistic power blocs, each of which came to see military success as a sign of divine favor. Therefore, in spite of intensive cultural exchanges, the prevalent attitude was one of hostility. Muslim armies conquered North Africa and Spain, crossing the Straits of Gibraltar in 711 and reaching as far as the French city of Tours by 732. Several centuries later, in 1453, the Ottoman Turks captured Constantinople; they reached the walls of Vienna in 1529. Echoes of the fears of Christendom may be found even today in Christian worship. The celebration of the Feast of the Transfiguration on August 6 commemorates the lifting of the Turkish siege of Belgrade on that day in 1456, and many continue to sing Martin Luther's hymn "Lord, keep us steadfast in thy Word / And curb the Turks' and papists' sword" (written after the Christians' defeat at Budapest in 1541), with only slight revisions.

Viewed from an Islamic perspective, Christians launched the Crusades as a "holy war," purportedly aimed at recapturing the Holy Places in Jerusalem (beginning in 1095 and lasting until 1291), and the same logic was at work in the *reconquista* of Spain (completed in 1492). Aggression by Christians continued as an adjunct to the European colonialism of the eighteenth and nineteenth centuries, bringing British rule to parts of the Near East — Egypt, the Sudan, and India — as well as Dutch rule in Indonesia and French rule in North Africa. The establishment of the modern state of Israel (1948) has been understood by many Muslims to be merely a continuation of this Western "crusading" history.

PAUL LÖFFLER AND MARK N. SWANSON

Islam as a Challenge to Christian Theology and Missionary Activity

Besides posing geopolitical challenges to Christian empires, Islam has also posed theological challenges to Christian faith. The new faith arose in a region where Judaism and Christianity were known, and it claimed to be the culmination of a salvation history in which the older faiths figured: Moses and Jesus were prophets and apostles in a line that culminated in Muhammad, "the Seal of the Prophets," while the scripture revealed to Muhammad, the Qur'an, confirmed previous revelations, including the Torah *(Tawrât)* sent down to Moses and the Gospel *(Injîl)* sent down to Jesus. The Islamic revelation thus allowed a certain legitimacy to the Jewish and Christian communities (they were "people of the Book," "people of Scripture"), although the Qur'an and the developing Islamic tradition were also sharply critical of Jewish and Christian "distortions" in their beliefs, including the Christian worship of Jesus as Lord and God. In the light of Islam's clearly delineated monotheism *(tawhîd),* Christian teachings about the triunity of God and the incarnation of the Son of God were immediately suspect, as were Christian practices such as the veneration of the cross and images. Furthermore, the portrayal of Jesus that emerges from the Qur'an — an apostle of Islam whom, it appears, God took up into heaven to save from an ignominious death by crucifixion — is obviously at odds with the portrayal of Jesus in the Gospels of the Christian Bible.

The rapid Islamic conquest of so much of the historical heartland of the Christian movement posed a theological problem to the church of the seventh and eighth centuries and resulted in much soul-searching and finger-pointing at sins and heresies that might have provoked God's wrath, but Christian thinkers were slow to grasp Islam *itself* as a challenge to Christian thought. Thus the church father John of Damascus (d. ca. 750) was able to classify Islam as merely a recent Christian heresy. John's casual and contemptuous dismissal of "the still-prevailing deceptive superstition of the Ishmaelites, the forerunner of the Antichrist" was characteristic of many early Greek and Latin writings on the subject, some of which amounted to little more than war propaganda. These works often treated Islam as merely a form of idolatry; indeed, until 1180, converts from Islam to Christianity in Byzantium were required to anathematize "the god of Muhammad." Islam was frequently explained in apocalyptic terms; for example, in the late twelfth century Joachim of Fiore (d. 1202) identified the fourth head of the dragon of the book of Revelation with Muhammad, and the sixth head with Saladin (Salâh-al-dîn, d. 1193), who had recently (in 1187) recaptured Jerusalem from the Crusaders. In the Latin West wild stories about Muhammad and the genesis of Islam were eagerly related without examination, since, as Guibert of Nogent, writing before 1112, notes, "it is safe to speak evil of one whose malignity exceeds whatever ill can be spoken."

Although the West's knowledge of Islam grew in the centuries that followed (see below), sharp antitheses between Christianity and Islam continued to be drawn by many of the Reformers (e.g., Luther's derogatory remarks about Muhammad and the Qur'an), by early Protestant mission theology (for which Islam, being post-Christian, was seen as anti-Christian), and by some currents of dialectical theology (in which Islam is to be respected but is still judged to be mere religion in contrast to the biblical revelation, a view held by Hendrik Kraemer). The antitheses are still very strongly stressed by some contemporary Christians, especially some conservative Protestants (not only in the West but now throughout the world) who continue to hold very negative assessments of Islam. A somewhat different attitude was found among Arabic-speaking Christian theologians who, in writings from the late eighth century onward, attempted to convince Muslims of the intellectual respectability of Christian faith (i.e., that Christian doctrines of the Trinity and of the incarnation were not merely forms of tritheism and idolatry), and even more to persuade Christians to remain within the Christian community (a task in which they were only partially successful, to judge from the wave of conversions to Islam in the ninth and tenth centuries). These Arabophone theologians diligently sought out common ground upon which apologies for Christian faith could be built. They all used the word "Allah" without reservation to refer to the Christian God.

A church leader such as the Nestorian catholicos Timothy (d. 823) could make a carefully nuanced affirmation that Muhammad had "walked in the path of the prophets." Writers such as Theodore Abû-Qurra, Habîb Abû-Râ'ita, and 'Ammâr al-Basrî (all active early in the ninth century) were skilled in using Qur'anic vocabulary and content and were able to address Muslim dialectical theologians *(mutakallimûn)* in their own idiom. To these names may be added Hunayn-ibn-Ishâq (d. 873) and Yahyâ-ibn-'Adi (d. 974) as examples of important participants in the great projects of translating Greek philosophy and science into Arabic and the creation of a tradition of Arabic philosophy *(falsafa)* (see "Islamic Philosophy," chapter 6). As a result of this activity, Arabic-speaking intellectuals came to share a common language and a common canon of philosophical and scientific literature to which an apologist might appeal. Thus was established an Arabic Christian apologetic tradition that has continued up to today, one that may continue to give inspiration to Middle Eastern Christian communities that have survived over the centuries, coexisting with Muslims and making major cultural contributions, despite the vicissitudes of life under Islamic rule (see below).

Contemporary with the development of an Arabic Christian apologetic tradition is the development of an Islamic "refutation of the Christians'" literature, which developed the Qur'anic critique of Christian teaching and practice mentioned above. This literature fulfilled a variety of functions: it warned against trends in Islamic teaching and practice that could be considered Christianizing; it played a role in the making and "catechizing" of converts; and in its early decades it assured Muslims of the superiority of their faith, despite what at first was the greater intellectual sophistication of their Christian subjects. Some of this literature displays a very good grasp of Christian teachings (and divisions) and responds to them with impressive dialectic (e.g., by al-Warrâq [d. ca. 861], al-Nâshi' al-Akbar [d. 906], al-Bâqillânî [d. 1013], and Ibn-Taymiyya [d. 1328]). The literature is also interesting for its varied treatments of Christian scripture, which is sometimes utilized, though transposed into an Islamic key (e.g., by al-Qâsim-ibn-Ibrâhîm [d. ca. 860] and ʿAlî-ibn-Rabbân al-Tabarî [d. ca. 860]), and sometimes attacked for its internal contradictions and general unreliability (e.g., by Ibn-Hazm [d. 1064]).

A number of issues that would be important for the subsequent history of Christian-Muslim relations were raised in the medieval Christian West. The need for a greater understanding of Islam was perceived and addressed, a notable example being the translation project of Peter the Venerable, abbot of Cluny, which included the 1143 Latin Qur'an translation of Robert Ketton (d. ca. 1160). Similar ventures grace the following centuries and are dramatically illustrated by Luther's defense of Theodore Bibliander's (d. 1564) publication of a Latin translation of the Qur'an in Basel in 1543.

St. Francis of Assisi (d. 1226) and the Franciscans pioneered a nonviolent missionary approach to the Muslims; a weirdly brilliant Franciscan tertiary, Ramon Llull (d. ca. 1315), was a champion of noncoercive rational apologetic. The Benedictine monk Uthred of Boldon (d. 1390), at Oxford in the 1360s, explored possibilities for the salvation of non-Christians; although his opinions on the matter were censured, his idea that an individual's destiny-deciding encounter with God takes place at the moment of death was picked up by others, such as John Wycliffe (d. 1384). After the fall of Constantinople, Nicholas of Cusa (d. 1464) imagined a heavenly Christian-Muslim dialogue through which Christians could explain their faith; his friend John of Segovia (d. 1458) did his utmost to make such a dialogue *(contraferentia)* an earthly reality. It was the same Nicholas who, in his *Sifting of the Qur'an,* affirmed that the Qur'an contains truth. Christian scholars of Islam and missionary thinkers of the twentieth century would revisit all these issues.

The age of Protestant Christian missions is marked by a number of initiatives aimed at bringing the gospel to Muslims throughout the world. It should be noted at the outset that neither Catholic nor Protestant missionary work among Muslims has led any great number to baptism, partly because of the Islamic "law of apostasy" prohibiting conversion out of the Islamic community. However, the missionaries' work in countries throughout the world — frequently under colonial protection — enabled Christian values, philosophy, and culture to exert an indirect influence. In particular, extensive educational work has been very significant in the formation of Muslim elites.

Specific missionaries who deserve mention include Henry Martyn (d. 1812), Karl Gottlieb Pfander (d. 1865), Thomas Valpy French (d. 1891), and Lewis Bevan Jones (d. 1960). While these persons were endowed from the beginning with great linguistic and intellectual gifts and love for individuals, their work moved from a reliance on the controversial method (especially marked in the case of Pfander) to a dialogic approach that takes Islam seriously as a context within which to pursue the Christian theological task (especially Jones and the Henry Martyn School/Institute, of which he was the first principal). The American Reformed missionary Samuel M. Zwemer (d. 1952) may have done more than any other individual to generate the interest of Western Protestant churchgoers in majority Muslim areas in the world. Anglican missions in the Near East contributed a special character of thoughtfulness and a desire to understand Islam "from the inside," a tradition graced by figures such as Temple Gairdner (d. 1928), Constance Padwick (d. 1968), and Kenneth Cragg. Cragg, whose seminal *The Call of the Minaret* (1956) has been followed by dozens of other elegantly written books, has exerted an enormous influence on Protestant missionary thinking and practice in relation to Islam in the second half of the twentieth century. Many other Protestant theologians have made major contributions to the theology of religions, the respectful Christian study of

Islam, and the practice of Christian-Muslim dialogue, including William Montgomery Watt (d. 1996), Wilfred Cantwell Smith (d. 2000), and Willem A. Bijlefeld.

The towering figure in the development of Catholic attitudes toward Islam in the twentieth century is the French scholar of Islam Louis Massignon (d. 1962), who in his teaching, hundreds of publications, and life full of activity on behalf of Muslims explored the spiritual kinship between the two faiths and probed the mystery of Islam's place in God's providence. His influence is plain to see in the large number of Catholic thinkers who have drawn inspiration from him, and especially in documents of the Second Vatican Council (1962-1965). *Lumen Gentium* 16 explicitly states that the Muslims are included in "the plan of salvation," while *Nostra Aetate* 3 begins with the deceptively simple yet revolutionary statement that the church "looks with esteem upon" the Muslims and ends with a call for Christians and Muslims to strive for mutual understanding and to work together on behalf of all humankind. Other names that should be mentioned here include Massignon's disciples Youakim Mubarac (d. 1994) and Guilio Basetti-Sani, the Dominicans Jacques Jomier (d. 2008) and Georges Anawati (d. 1994), the Père Blanc Robert Caspar (d. 2007), and the academic theologian Hans Küng.

Christian-Muslim Engagement Today

Islamic history is in general characterized by tolerance toward communities of Christians and Jews, communities that have enjoyed freedom of worship and that have ordered their affairs according to their own laws of "personal status." At certain times and places there have been creative interaction and cooperation, and even theological discussion, between communities. This tolerance is dictated by the Qur'an itself, which not only prohibits coercion in matters of religion but positively enjoins respect for Jews and Christians as "people of the Book" — even though, as we have seen, the Qur'an also criticizes what it views as Christian and Jewish exaggerations or excesses in their beliefs.

A practical difficulty in intercommunal relations is that Islamic tolerance does not in theory allow for the possibility of conversion from Islam to any other religious community (see the Islamic Declaration of Human Rights of 1981). In contrast, conversion to Islam is encouraged and welcomed, with demographic results that are obvious in the (once Christian)

Middle East and North Africa. Another pressing issue is the place of non-Muslims in Islamic states. Can Christians, for example, be full cocitizens of such a state, or will they have the status of *dhimmîs* (protected persons)? Muslim minorities in Western countries have analogous concerns: Can their members live as Muslims and pass their faith on to their children in secularized Western societies?

During the final third of the twentieth century, "dialogue" has been a key concept for thinking about new and renewed approaches in Christian-Muslim relations. Building on the developments adumbrated above, possibilities for dialogue have been explored by the Roman Catholic Church's Secretariat for Non-Christians (established in 1964), which in 1988 became the Pontifical Council on Interreligious Dialogue (PCID), and by the World Council of Churches, which sponsored its first formal Christian-Muslim dialogue in 1969 in Cartigny, Switzerland, and two years later established a program subunit, Dialogue with People of Living Faiths and Ideologies. These efforts have helped to establish a new climate for dealing with both theological and practical problems. In frequent formal meetings between Muslim and Christian leaders, theological and spiritual issues have been discussed, as well as common concerns about human rights and dignity (the protection of minorities, religious liberty, peacemaking, justice for oppressed peoples, and so on) and the practice of Islamic *da'wa* ("call" or "summons") and Christian mission including issues concerning proselytism, diaconal work, and the entanglement of Christian mission with Western imperialism.

The present situation is full of complexity. Muslim communities continue to grow in once-predominantly Christian countries; clashes involving Christians and Muslims continue to occur with sad regularity in various parts of the world; the vigorous revival of Islam in many Muslim majority areas in the world brings an increasingly self-confident and assertive presence to Christian-Muslim relations; and Christians continue to hold widely divergent views on the proper "approach" to Muslims. Dialogue is certainly here to stay, the reality and risk of conflict in some parts of the world making it a critical component of building both community and nation. But it has gradually become apparent that the most effective dialogue is not that carried out at major international conferences but that which takes place at the local level and which focuses on very concrete challenges and problems. In many places (e.g., Egypt, Pakistan, and Indonesia) there has been fruitful interaction between Christian and Muslim intellectuals on matters of human rights, the development of civil society, and other areas, while at the grassroots level Christians and Muslims have worked together to promote health, literacy, and economic development.

Another area for Christian reflection and dialogue involves recognition of the continuing theological and ethical challenges of Islam. A growing number of Western Christian theologians in the current intellectual climate (of, e.g., postmodern and ecumenical theology) are beginning to appreciate the importance of other faith traditions such as Islam — and not just Western philosophies — as major dialogue partners. As Christian theologians in Muslim countries gain a voice, they too (in continuity with the Arabophone theologians mentioned above) point the way to new possibilities for elaborating a Christian dialogic theology in relation to Islam.

Chapter Fifteen

ISLAM IN AMERICA

Jane I. Smith

Muslims in the United States and Canada represent a great many movements and identities: immigrant and indigenous, Sunni and Shi'ite, conservative and liberal. While exact numbers are difficult to determine, most estimates for the early twenty-first century assume that there are well over four million, perhaps as many as six million, Muslims in North America.

Immigrants

The majority of American Muslims are: immigrants who arrived in the United States after the enactment of the 1965 Immigration and Nationalities Act that abolished national origins quotas, their descendants, and the descendants of the immigrants who first began to arrive in the West in the latter part of the nineteenth century. The early arrivals, comprising mainly laborers and merchants, settled in the East, the Midwest, and on the Pacific coast. Other waves of immigration occurred as a direct result of political and economic circumstances in the Arab world and in countries with large Muslim populations, including the breakup of the Ottoman Empire, the partition of India, the Israeli defeat of the Palestinians, the Iranian revolution, and uprisings in Africa and Asia. Important too were developments in the West, such as the civil rights movement. Initially coming mainly from the Middle East, immigrants in the last decades of the twentieth century came from majority-Muslim areas all over the world, from Bosnia to Bangladesh, from Mauritania to Myanmar. While the first arrivals generally were not well trained or economically advantaged, Muslims today are often among the most highly educated and professionally successful Americans.

In earlier decades, because their numbers were relatively small, immigrant Muslims were forced to come together in mixed groups for worship and social interaction. As more arrived and settled in various parts of the country, national and ethnic groups were able to meet and worship separately. These associations continue, although with the rise in consciousness of being Muslim in the North American context, more immigrant Muslims of differing nationalities are living in proximity and worshiping together. Shi'ites, who account for about one-fifth of the American Muslim community, observe some rites and holidays distinct from Sunnis and usually worship separately.

African-Americans

Growing numbers of Muslims in the United States are African-American. In the early decades of the twentieth century, several black religious movements began to claim Islamic roots and identity. The Nation of Islam became the most prominent African-American freedom movement to identify with Islam, beginning in Detroit in the 1930s under the leadership of the Honorable Elijah Muhammad. Many of the teachings of the Nation are irreconcilable with traditional Islam, including recognition of the prophethood of Elijah and the promotion of racial separatism. Political disagreements led the prominent and popular minister Malcolm X, one of the Nation's most influential spokesmen, to leave the organization in 1964. Shortly thereafter, he performed the pilgrimage to Mecca, or Hajj. He was assassinated in 1965.

Meanwhile the Nation continued to grow. When Elijah Muhammad died in 1975, he was succeeded by his son Wallace. The new leadership brought momentous changes as the political millenarianism of the earlier Nation gave way to a visible move toward orthodox Islam. Wallace, who changed his name to Wârith Deen Mohammed (d. 2008), played down the nationalism that had characterized the preaching of both his father and Malcolm, focusing on Islam as a spiritual force rather than a political tool. His organization, the name of which has evolved a number of times, is now called the Muslim American Society, and its members no longer consider themselves part of the Nation, but simply Sunni Muslims. African-Americans, including those belonging to mainstream Sunni groups as well as a number of sectarian groups, constitute some 30 percent of the Muslim community in America.

The Nation of Islam itself is now under the leadership of Minister Louis Farrakhan, who first came to prominence as the minister of a mosque in Harlem, where he succeeded Malcolm X when the latter left the Nation in 1964. In 1977 Farrakhan broke with Wârith Deen Mohammed, leader of what was then called the World Community of Islam, in order to rebuild Elijah Muhammad's Lost-Found Nation of Islam in the Wilderness of America. Since then, Minister Farrakhan has become a celebrated and controversial figure within American society, largely as a result of his perceived racism and anti-Semitism. He has, however, succeeded in reconstructing the Nation of Islam and in recent years has shown an ability to bring various segments of the African-American Muslim community together and thus has helped that community find a place within the pluralistic world of American religion.

Converts

A third grouping of American Muslims, far smaller than the immigrants or African-Americans, is made up of others who have decided to adopt Islam as a faith and an identity. These Muslims include people associated with Sufi movements, women who change their faith on marriage, some who find Islam intellectually persuasive, and growing numbers of Hispanics and Native Americans. The *da'wa* (literally "call, summons"), or Islamic missionary movement, is strong in America, and Muslims are active in making conversions in prisons, in the academic world, and in various minority communities.

Mosques

For many decades Muslims in America functioned with little or no trained leadership and without their own designated space for meeting and worship. Several places claim to be the site of the first American mosque, most notably Cedar Rapids, Iowa, and Ross, North Dakota. Other mosques were built in New York, Massachusetts, and the Midwest in the 1920s and 1930s. The mosque movement began to gain momentum by the middle of the century, highlighted by the completion of the Islamic Center in Washington, D.C., in 1957. Toward the end of the twentieth century much of the funding for building Islamic establishments, as well as for providing trained leadership for Muslim congregations, came from oil-producing countries of the Middle East. Flourishing Islamic communities are now found in most major cities of the United States, and the number of mosques and Islamic centers has grown enormously. They provide a range of activities aside from worship, including after-school education, libraries, gymnasiums, facilities for the elderly, and contexts for social engagement. Many Muslim groups, especially African-American congregations, for whom finances remain a major consideration, continue to worship and meet in much smaller facilities such as converted houses or storefronts.

While some imams trained overseas provide leadership to American mosques, their numbers are insufficient, and their training is often inadequate to meet the concerns of life in America. Significant efforts are under way to educate an indigenous leadership. American imams are called on to function in capacities well beyond what is expected in Islamic societies. Paralleling the roles of Christian and Jewish clergy, imams not only preach and teach but also provide counseling, raise funds, perform weddings and funerals, educate the public about Islam, and participate in community projects. Trained imams and chaplains are increasingly present in the armed services and in the prison system, and the number of colleges and universities hiring Muslim chaplains is growing rapidly.

Organizations

Beginning in the 1960s with the establishment of the Muslim Student Association, America has seen a steady growth of Muslim organizations at the local and national levels. Some are specific to professions and interests, while others serve as umbrella organizations. Of the latter the two largest are ISNA, the Islamic Society of North America, and the somewhat smaller and more conservative ICNA, Islamic Circle of North America. Important also is the recently formed MANA, Muslim Alliance in North America. Organizations such as the Washington D.C.–based Council on American-Islamic Relations (CAIR) exist to advance the political presence of Muslims in America, to support civil rights and women's rights, and to spread accurate information about Islam in the effort to combat anti-Muslim prejudice. The national Muslim Youth of North America and many local groups sponsor summer gatherings and work opportunities for teenagers.

Some of the Muslim organizations publish journals with articles designed to help Muslims live Islamically in the context of what they see as an essentially secular society. These journals, along with growing resources on the Internet, services provided by mosques and local communities, and the large amount of literature and media information available on Islam, offer a range of solutions to the concerns of everyday life. These concerns include raising and educating children, dating and marriage, women in the workplace, appropriate dress for men and women, participation in the American economic system, observing daily prayer rituals in the public sphere, and maintaining proper Islamic diet. Some Muslims feel that the best way to maintain their Islamic identity in America is to avoid contact as much as possible with those who are not Muslim, while others are equally convinced that full participation and involvement are not only appropriate but necessary.

Prospects

Muslims in America are in the process of determining the nature and validity of an indigenous American Islam. Immigrant Muslim communities are subject to a range of international influences, and they are struggling to determine when interpretations of Islam from different political and cultural contexts are appropriate to the practice of the faith in the West. Muslims who traditionally have not been active in American politics are increasingly aware of the potential for political power, and many are working to build coalitions and political action committees to sponsor Muslim candidates and support Muslim causes. As the children and grandchildren of immigrant Muslims find themselves increasingly distant from their international cultural heritage, they are engaging in the task of emphasizing commonality over distinctiveness. They also acknowledge that the creation of an American *umma,* or community, must result in bringing together immigrant and indigenous Muslims, converts and those with a long heritage of Islam. To the extent to which they succeed, American Muslims believe they will be able to contribute significantly to the international discourse about Islam in the contemporary world and the role to be played in it by Muslims.

Glossary

Terms printed in bold have their own entries in this glossary.

Abbasids (750-1258) A dynasty of caliphs that ruled from their capital Baghdad (founded 762) from 750, when they overthrew the **Umayyads**, till 1258, when the Mongols sacked Baghdad.

Abû-Bakr (d. 634) A close Companion of **Muhammad**, later Muhammad's father-in-law, and after Muhammad's death, the first caliph of the Muslim community (632-634).

Abû-Hanîfa (d. 767) Early Baghdadi jurist (or legal scholar) for whom the **Hanafîs**, one of the four Sunni *madhhabs* ("schools of legal thought"), are named.

Abû-Tâlib (d. 619) One of Muhammad's uncles who did not convert but who provided protection for his nephew. He was the father of ʿAlî.

adhân Arabic word for the "call to prayer," called out from the top of mosque **minarets** by a muezzin and now also broadcast on radio and television, and programmed on computers and hand-held devices.

ahl al-bayt Literally "people of the house," the term refers to the members of **Muhammad**'s family. For **Shiʿites**, the term refers only to Muhammad, his daughter **Fâtima**, her husband ʿAlî, and their children Hasan and **Husayn**.

ahl al-kitâb Literally "people of the Book" or "people of Scripture." This is a

Qur'anic term for those people who follow the scriptures revealed by God before Islam, in common usage principally Jews and Christians.

Ahmad-ibn-Hanbal (d. 855) A Baghdadi jurist known for his austerity and rejection of **Mu'tazilî** notions about the **Qur'an**'s so-called createdness. The Hanbalî *madhhab,* one of the four Sunni "schools of legal thought," is named for him.

'Â'isha (d. 678) Daughter of **Abû-Bakr** and one of **Muhammad**'s later wives, who transmitted numerous **hadiths**.

'Alî-ibn-Abî-Tâlib (d. 661) Cousin of **Muhammad**, later his son-in-law, one of the first converts to Islam, and fourth caliph (656-661). **Shi'ites** regard him as the first **Imam**, that is, Muhammad's direct spiritual successor. For Sunnis, he is one of the four "rightly-guided caliphs."

Allâh Arabic word for "God," like *Dios* in Spanish or *Dieu* in French.

Ansâr Literally "Helpers," the name given to the inhabitants of **Medina** who welcomed **Muhammad** and the Meccans who followed him.

al-Ash'arî (d. 935) A *kalâm* (dialectical) theologian whose views about God's attributes became influential in elaboration of Sunni theology generally.

'asr Name of the midafternoon ritual prayer.

awliyâ' (**sing.** *walî*) Literally "friends," a term used to describe figures akin to saints, because of the favor they are believed to find with God.

âya (**pl.** *âyât*) Literally "sign," and used to refer to God's signs, to the verses of the **Qur'an**, and in **Twelver** Shi'ism to the highest-ranking clerics in the title Ayatollah (*âyat Allah,* "sign of God").

baraka God's grace, believed by many to emanate also from *awliyâ'* (saints).

Bayt Allâh "House of God," one of the names of the **Ka'ba**.

da'wa Literally "call" or "summons," the word used to describe any activity directed toward educating non-Muslims about Islam, or toward converting them to Islam.

dhikr Literally "mentioning," devotional repeating of pious phrases or Qur'anic passages, engaged in by all observant Muslims, and an especially important part of **Sufi** practice.

dhimmî A person who is guaranteed protection under the *dhimma,* "pact of protection." A reference to members of the *ahl al-kitâb*, practitioners of revealed religions other than Islam.

fajr Name of the predawn ritual prayer.

falsafa Arabic word for Greek philosophy.

Fâtiha "The Opening," the name of the first chapter in the printed **Qur'an**.

Fâtima (d. 632) One of **Muhammad**'s four daughters, the wife of ʿAlî, mother of Hasan and **Husayn**, and a key figure of the *ahl al-bayt*. The Shiʿite Fâtimid dynasty (909-1171) is named for her.

fatwâ (pl. *fatâwâ*) For Sunnis the nonbinding legal opinion of a jurist *(mufti)*; for Shiʿites, the judicial decision of a jurist *mujtahid*.

fiqh Literally "understanding," the term used for the law or for jurisprudence. A jurist is thus called a *faqîh;* legal theory is called *usûl al-fiqh* (literally "the roots of understanding"); and substantive law is called *furûʿ al-fiqh* ("the branches of understanding").

al-Ghazâlî (d. 1111) A professor of law and theology at the Nizâmiyya Madrasa (Law College) in Baghdad whose critique of philosophy led to an influential synthesis of *kalâm* (dialectical theology), *falsafa* (Greek philosophy), and Sufism (mysticism).

hadith, Hadith Literally "speech," a report of **Muhammad**'s actions, statements, and practices that received his tacit approval. In common English usage, lowercase "hadith" refers to an individual report (frequently translated "[prophetic] tradition") and uppercase "Hadith" to the entire corpus ("Tradition").

Hajj The pilgrimage to **Mecca** at the prescribed time, in the twelfth month of the Islamic calendar (Dhûl-Hijja); one of the "pillars" of Islam.

halâl Any act "permissible" under Islamic law, popularly used to describe food conforming to dietary regulations.

Hanafî One of the four Sunni "schools of legal thought," inspired by the legal methodology of its eponym, **Abû Hanîfa**; also an adherent of that "school."

Hanbalî One of the four Sunni *madhhabs* ("schools of legal thought") based on the legal methodology of its eponym, **Ahmad-ibn-Hanbal**; also the term for an adherent of that "school."

harâm "Prohibited," used in connection with acts and also the popularly used term to describe prohibited food and drink; found also in the expression *al-Masjid al-Harâm,* "Sacred Mosque," referring to the Grand Mosque in Mecca.

hijâb Head covering or hair covering worn by many Muslim women (distinct from the veil, covering the face, worn by very few Muslim women).

Hijra Literally "migration," the name given to the emigration of **Muhammad** and his followers (the *Muhâjirûn*) from **Mecca** to **Medina** in 622. The Islamic calendar commences with the Hijra and is thus called the Hijrî calendar.

Husayn (or al-Husayn) (d. 680) The younger of **Muhammad**'s two grandsons through his daughter **Fâtima** and her husband, Muhammad's cousin, 'Alî; the third **Shi'ite Imam,** martyred at Karbala (in present-day Iraq) by the forces of the **Umayyad** caliph Yazîd (ruled 680-683). Shi'ites commemorate Husayn's death with mourning in Muharram, the first month of the Islamic calendar.

Ibn-Rushd (Averroës, d. 1198) A polymath of Muslim Spain and North Africa, whose works on Plato and Aristotle were influential in both Islamic and European philosophy.

Ibn-Sîna (Avicenna, d. 1037) The most important medieval Islamic philosopher and scientist, whose medical works were also extremely influential in Europe.

'Îd al-Adhâ "Feast of Sacrifice," celebrated on the tenth day of the pilgrimage month, on which pilgrims outside **Mecca** sacrifice animals in ritual reenactment of Abraham's willingness to sacrifice his son. Muslims not on pilgrimage participate in a congregational morning prayer and also sacrifice animals. In both cases, meat is distributed to the needy.

'Îd al-Fitr "Feast of Fast-Breaking," celebrated on the first day of Shawwâl, the month following Ramadan, marking the end of the monthlong fasting the preceding month. There are a congregational morning prayer and typically visits to family and friends, and gift giving, especially to children.

ihrâm Name of the **Hajj** or *'umra* pilgrims' attire, and also the name for the sacralized state that attire represents; for men it consists of two pieces of unsewn white cloth, for women simple garments.

ihsân Virtue (literally "making beautiful"), described by **Muhammad** in one celebrated **hadith** as a believer acting as if she can see God, and knowing with certitude that God sees her.

i'jâz (al-Qur'ân) Inimitability (of the **Qur'an**), the notion that the Qur'an, as the word of God, is miraculous and irreproducible.

ijâza Literally "authorization." In Sufism a "certificate of graduation" granted by the master to the disciple.

ijmâ' Consensus among jurists on a question of law or jurisprudence.

ijtihâd Legal reasoning exercise by a jurist (literally "exertion").

imam Prayer leader, in Sunnism any male having reached puberty and of sound mind. In Shi'ism, the title given to the spiritual successors of **Muhammad**, and deferentially also to high-ranking clerics.

Injîl "Evangel" or Gospel of Jesus ('Îsâ), mentioned in the **Qur'an** as one of the preceding scriptures or "books"; Christians are thus included as *ahl al-kitâb*, "people of the book."

'Îsâ-ibn-Maryam Jesus, almost always referred to in the **Qur'an** as Jesus, son of Mary, a major prophet, and therefore a man, not divine.

'ishâ' Name of the nighttime ritual prayer.

Ja'far al-Sâdiq (d. 765) Important early pious figure, religious scholar, and, for Shi'ites, the sixth Imam; a quietist who enjoined moderation.

jâmi' Congregational mosque, used for Friday ritual congregational prayers.

jihâd "Struggle" in the cause of religion, understood to mean everything from pious striving (e.g., charity) and religious striving (e.g., teaching the **Qur'an**), to armed struggle, whence the term *mujâhidîn* (literally "strugglers") applied famously to those resisting the Soviet invasion of Afghanistan (1979-1989).

Jum'a (also Jumu'a) "Friday," shorthand for the Friday Congregational Prayer.

Ka'ba Cube-shaped, hollow stone shrine in **Mecca** to which Arabs before Islam made pilgrimage, and which Muslims circumambulate during their pilgrimages to it. Muslims believe it was built by Adam and rebuilt by Abraham. **Muhammad** oriented prayer toward it *(qibla)* and emptied it of its idols.

kalâm Dialectical or speculative theology, philosophical speculation about theologial matters.

Khadîja (d. 619) Muhammad's widowed employer, then wife of twenty-five years, was the first convert and an important support for him. Muhammad's only children who survived to adulthood were their four daughters, Zaynab, Ruqayya, Umm Kulthûm, and Fâtima.

khalîfa **(pl.** *khulafâ*') Caliph, the title applied by Sunnis to **Muhammad's** successors. The first four are called "the rightly-guided caliphs" *(al-khulafâ' al-râshidûn),* namely, **Abû-Bakr,** 'Umar, 'Uthmân, and 'Alî.

khânqâh Residential **Sufi** lodge. The word is Persian; its equivalent in Arabic is *ribât.*

madhhab Sunni school of legal thought or jurisprudence. There are four *madhhab*s, though initially, in the ninth century, there were many.

madrasa Medieval residential college of law, created by private pious endowment, for the training of jurists. Today, the term is used to describe a regular school or a seminary.

maghrib Name of the sunset ritual prayer.

Mahdî Literally "guided one," a reference to the messianic figure who will emerge in the end-time to help establish just rule on earth. For **Shi'ites,** the title of the returning **Imam.**

Mâlikî One of the four Sunni *madhhab*s ("schools of legal thought") based on the legal methodology of its eponym, **Mâlik-ibn-Anas;** also the term for an adherent of that school.

Mâlik-ibn-Anas (d. ca. 795) Early jurist and eponym of the **Mâlikî** school of legal thought.

Maryam Mary, mother of Jesus ('Îsâ), for whom a Qur'anic chapter is named. She is in popular belief one of the four women guaranteed paradise, the other three being Âsiya (the adoptive mother of Mûsâ [Moses]), **Muhammad's** wife, **Khadîja,** and their daughter, **Fâtima.**

masjid Mosque, place of daily congregational prayer, usually a building founded through a pious endowment *(waqf).*

al-Mâturîdî (d. 944) Eponym of one of three important Sunni schools of dialectical (or speculative) theology *(kalâm).*

Mecca *Makka al-Mukarrama,* "Mecca the Blessed," trading and pilgrimage city in western Arabia, site of an ancient shrine (see **Ka'ba**), sometime home of

Abraham, Hagar, and Ishmael, and birthplace of **Muhammad** (570) and Islam (610).

Medina *Madîna al-Munawwara,* "Medina the Radiant," city in western Arabia, north of **Mecca,** to which **Muhammad** and the nascent Muslim community emigrated (**Hijra**) in 622 to flee persecution by **Quraysh**-controlled **Mecca.**

mihrâb Marker for the direction of prayer, often rendered in the form of a niche placed in the center of the *qibla* wall in a mosque.

minaret Place used for the call to prayer, typically a tower.

minbar Pulpit in a mosque used for religious sermons, most commonly consisting of a few steps and an elevated seat.

Mi'râj The ascension of **Muhammad** to the heavens from Jerusalem, astride the winged creature Burâq, and in the company of Jibrîl (Gabriel). It followed Muhammad's *Isrâ'* (Night Journey) from **Mecca** to Jerusalem. Most Muslims regard these journeys as physical, some as spiritual.

Mu'âwiya (d. 680) Opponent of 'Alî, the fourth caliph, he became the fifth caliph, and effectively the first caliph of the **Umayyad** dynasty. He was succeeded by his son, Yazîd.

Muhâjirûn Emigrants. The term is used to describe those who emigrated from **Mecca** to **Medina** with **Muhammad** during the **Hijra** in 622.

Muhammad (570-632) "The Messenger of God," Prophet of Islam, born in **Mecca,** and deceased in **Medina.**

mujtahid One who exercises legal reasoning *(ijtihâd).* For Sunnis, one of the early authoritative jurists, such as the eponyms of the four Sunni *madhhabs,* though many reformists hold that any trained jurist can be a *mujtahid.* For **Shi'ites,** a *mujtahid* is a high-ranking expert jurist whose teachings must be adhered to.

Mûsâ The prophet Moses, who figures prominently and at great length in the **Qur'an.**

Mu'tazilî Adherent of a prominent school of dialectical theology *(kalâm),* one celebrated position of which is the belief in the "createdness" of the **Qur'an.**

nabî Prophet (of God).

qâdî Judge.

qibla The direction of the Ka'ba (in **Mecca**) in ritual prayer.

Qur'an Literally "Recitation," the scripture of Islam, believed by Muslims to have been revealed by God to **Muhammad** in Arabic through the archangel Jibrîl (Gabriel). It is regarded as liturgically valid only in Arabic, inimitable (see *i'jâz*), and immutable.

Quraysh The influential tribe of **Mecca**, into one of whose clans **Muhammad** was born.

rasûl Messenger (of God).

Sahâba (sing. *Sahâbî*) The Companions of **Muhammad**, male and female. Although it can be applied to anyone who met Muhammad, it is generally used to describe his closest companions and disciples.

salafî Literally "predecessor," a reference to the conduct of **Muhammad**'s Companions *(Sahâba)* and the generations that followed them (Tâbi'în), regarded as superior to successive ones. The term is applied (sometimes inaccurately) to contemporary conservative and neoconservative Muslims.

salât Ritual prayer, one of the "pillars" of Islam, to be performed five times during the day *(fajr, zuhr, 'asr, maghrib, 'ishâ')*, everyday.

salawât God's blessings, in particular those wished or "called" upon the prophets **Muhammad** and Abraham (Ibrâhîm).

sawm (also *siyâm*) "Fast," abstention from food, drink, and sexual intercourse from before first light till sunset. Fasting the month of Ramadan is one of the "pillars" of Islam; voluntary pious fasting is permitted throughout the year except on the two high holidays, 'Îd al-Adhâ and 'Îd al-Fitr.

al-Shâfi'î (d. 820) Early jurist and author of the earliest treatise on legal hermeneutics; eponym of the **Shâfi'î** school of legal thought.

Shâfi'î One of the four Sunni *madhhab*s ("schools of legal thought"); based on the legal methodology of its eponym, **al-Shâfi'î**; also the term for an adherent of that school.

shahâda The "testimony" of faith, consisting in reciting the phrase "I testify that there is no god (worthy of worship) other than God and I testify that Muhammad is His Servant and Messenger."

147

Sharî'a Islamic law, but properly, revealed religious law.

shaykh Literally "elder," the title given to a **Sufi** guide or master; also a term of respect for any religious scholar or notable.

Shi'ite From *shî'î* ("partisan"), from *shî'at 'Alî* ("party" of **'Alî**). Broadly, any person who holds that the descendants of Muhammad have a privileged position and are his legitimate spiritual successors, called **Imams**. Today, the largest Shi'ite group is the **Twelvers** (or *Imâmîs*).

Sufi Loosely "mystic"; originally, an ascetic who renounced things worldly, later any person adopting certain practices of mystical piety (Sufism [*tasawwuf*]).

sultan *(sultân)* Literally "potentate," a title of temporal rule adopted by rulers beginning in the eleventh century.

Sunna Literally "custom" or "way," the practice of following the exemplary practice of **Muhammad**, which became a normative concept for Muslims.

sura "Chapter" of the **Qur'an**.

tafsîr Exegesis or commentary of the **Qur'an**.

tarîqa Institutionalized **Sufi** social groupings according to specific spiritual lineages going back in all cases but one — the Naqshbandiyya, which goes through **Abû-Bakr** — through 'Alî to **Muhammad**, for example, the Qâdiriyya.

tawhîd Term for the oneness, or indivisibility, of God.

Tawrât The Torah (Hebrew Bible), mentioned frequently in the **Qur'an** as one of the preceding scriptures or "books"; Jews are thus included as *ahl al-kitâb*, "people of the book."

Twelvers Largest group among the Shî'a, so called for the number of **Imams** they recognize; they are also known as *Imâmîs*.

'ulamâ' (sing. *'âlim*) Literally "knower," the term that came to be applied to a scholar of the religious sciences, and Anglicized as "ulema."

'Umar-ibn-al-Khattâb (d. 644) Close Companion of **Muhammad**, later his father-in-law, and after Muhammad's death, the first caliph of the Muslim community (634-644).

Umayyads (661-750) A caliphal dynasty, founded by **Mu'âwiya**, the fifth caliph, with its capital in Damascus. The Spanish Umayyads ruled in Spain, from 756 to 929 as emirs (princes) and from 929 to 1031 claiming the title caliph.

umma The totality of the community of Muslims.

'umra Voluntary pilgrimage to **Mecca** at any time during the year.

'Uthmân-ibn-'Affân (d. 656) Close Companion of **Muhammad**, later Muhammad's son-in-law, and after Muhammad's death, the third caliph of the Muslim community (644-656). He is credited with having collected the **Qur'an** into a single authorized version.

waqf (pl. *awqâf*) Religious endowment, usually charitable; it is through *awqâf* that mosques, law colleges, and shrines are built and maintained.

wudû' Ablution, the washing of the mouth, nostrils, face, forearms, and feet before prayer; in the absence of water, this ritual may be performed with earth (and is then called *tayammum*).

Zabûr Qur'anic term for the psalms of David.

zakât Obligatory 2.5 percent alms-tax on accumulated wealth, and one of the "pillars" of Islam.

ziyâra Visit to tombs, shrines, and holy places.

zuhr Name of the early afternoon ritual prayer.

Bibliography for Further Viewing and Reading

Documentaries

Islamic Conversations. Films for the Humanities, 1993. 6 × 30 minutes (DVD):
    Islam and Pluralism
    Islam and Christianity
    Islam and War
    The Islamic State
    Authority and Change
    Women and Islam
Living Islam. BBC TV, 1993. 6 × 50 minutes (VHS):
    Foundations
    Challenge of the Past
    Struggling with Modernity
    Paradise Lies at the Feet of the Mother
    Among the Non-Believers
    Last Crusade
When the World Spoke Arabic: The Golden Age of Arab Civilization. Films for the
    Humanities, 1999. 12 × 27 minutes (VHS/DVD):
    The Arabs Make Their Entrance: Islam and Empire
    Once upon a Time: Baghdad during the Abbasid Dynasty
    The Andalusian Epic: Islamic Spain
    They Surveyed the World: Exploring the Islamic Empire and Beyond
    The Muslim Town: Urban Life under the Caliphate
    An Art of Living: Arab Aesthetics in Ninth-Century Spain

The Secrets of the Human Body: Islam's Contributions to Medicine
Everything under the Sun: Astronomy, Mathematics, and Islam
The Thousand and One Nights: A Historical Perspective
Ulema and Philosophers: Faith vs. Reason in Islamic Arabia
From Arabic to Latin: The Assimilation of Arab Knowledge
Forgetting the Arabs: Europe on the Cusp of the Renaissance
Islam: Empire of Faith. PBS, 2001. 160 minutes (DVD).
Inside Islam. History Channel, 2002. 100 minutes (DVD).
Muhammad: Legacy of a Prophet. Unity Production, 2002. 120 minutes (DVD).
Frontline — Muslims. Frontline, 2002. 120 minutes (DVD).

Online

There is a great deal of misinformation on the Internet. The following are a selection of reliable Web sites and portals. These links were active at the time of compilation of this bibliography (November 2010).

http://web.me.com/gary_bunt/pathways/pathways.html — "Islamic Studies Pathways — an Academic Guide to Islamic Studies Resources on the Internet," maintained by Dr. Gary R. Bunt, University of Wales, Trinity Saint David.
http://www.oxfordislamicstudies.com — "Oxford Islamic Studies Online," maintained by Professor John L. Esposito, Georgetown University.
http://www.uga.edu/islam/ — "Islam and Islamic Studies Resource," maintained by Professor Alan Godlas, University of Georgia.
http://www.unc.edu/Ecernst/~resources.htm — "Resources for Islamic Studies and Related Subjects," maintained by Professor Carl Ernst, University of North Carolina, Chapel Hill.

Print

Selected full English translations of the Qur'an

There are upwards of seventy English-language translations of the Qur'an. The following are the ones we recommend. They represent a mix of translations preferred by Western scholars and Anglophone Muslims. If the translation is available online, we supply the link.
The Koran Interpreted: A Translation. Translated by A. J. Arberry. New York: Simon and Schuster, 1996. Available online at http://www.oxfordislamicstudies.com/.

The Meaning of the Glorious Koran: An Explanatory Translation. Translated by M. M. Pickthall. London: Everyman's Library, 1992 (1930). Available online at http://www.usc.edu/schools/college/crcc/engagement/resources/texts/muslim/quran/.

The Meaning of the Holy Qur'an. Translated by Abdullah Yusuf Ali. 10th rev. ed. Beltsville, Md.: Amana Publications, 1999 (1938). Available online at http://www.usc.edu/schools/college/crcc/engagement/resources/texts/muslim/quran/.

The Qur'ān. Translated by Alan Jones. Cambridge: Gibb Trust, 2007.

The Qur'ān: A New Translation. Translated by M. A. S. Abdel Haleem. Corrected ed. Oxford: Oxford University Press, 2008. Available online at http://www.oxfordislamicstudies.com/.

The Qur'ān: A New Translation. Translated by Tarif Khalidi. London and New York: Penguin Classics, 2008.

Reference Works

Ali, Kecia, and Oliver Leaman. *Islam: The Key Concepts.* New York: Routledge, 2008.

Cornell, Vincent J., gen. ed. *Voices of Islam.* 5 vols. Westport, Conn.: Praeger, 2007.

Elias, Jamal J., ed. *Key Themes for the Study of Islam.* Oxford: Oneworld, 2010.

Encyclopaedia of Islam. Edited by H. A. R. Gibb et al. 12 vols. 2nd ed. Leiden: Brill, 1954-2009.

Encyclopaedia of Islam and the Muslim World. Edited by Richard C. Martin. 2 vols. New York: Macmillan USA/ThomsonGale, 2004.

Encyclopaedia of the Qur'ān. Edited by J. D. McAuliffe. 5 vols. Leiden: Brill, 2001-2006.

Encyclopedia of Islam 3, The. Edited by Gudrun Krämer et al. Leiden: Brill, 2007-.

Ende, Werner, and Udo Steinbach. *Islam in the World Today: A Handbook of Politics, Religion, Culture, and Society.* Ithaca, N.Y.: Cornell University Press, 2010.

Glassé, Cyril. *The Concise Encyclopaedia of Islam.* 3rd ed. London: Stacey International, 2008.

Medieval Islamic Civilization: An Encyclopedia. Edited by Josef Meri. 2 vols. New York: Routledge, 2006.

Nanji, Azim. *The Penguin Dictionary of Islam.* London and New York, 2008.

New Cambridge History of Islam, The. Edited by Chase Robinson et al. 6 vols. Cambridge: Cambridge University Press, 2010.

Oxford Dictionary of Islam, The. Edited by John L. Esposito. New York: Oxford University Press, 2003.

Oxford Encyclopedia of the Islamic World. Edited by John L. Esposito. 6 vols. New York: Oxford University Press, 2009.

Renard, John, ed. *Windows on the House of Islam: Muslim Sources on Spirituality and Religious Life.* Berkeley: University of California Press, 1996.

Rippin, Andrew, and Jan Knappert, eds. and trans. *Textual Sources for the Study of Islam.* Chicago: University of Chicago Press, 1983.

Ruthven, Malise, with Azim Nanji. *Historical Atlas of Islam.* Cambridge: Harvard University Press, 2004.

Waldman, Marilyn R., and William H. McNeill, eds. *The Islamic World.* Chicago: University of Chicago Press, 1990.

Williams, John Alden. *Themes of Islamic Civilization.* Berkeley: University of California Press, 1971.

1. Islam

Arkoun, Mohammed. *Rethinking Islam: Common Questions, Uncommon Answers.* Translated and edited by Robert D. Lee. Boulder, Colo.: Westview Press, 1994.

Armstrong, Karen. *Muhammad: A Prophet for Our Time.* New York: Atlas Books/ HarperCollins, 2006.

Aslan, Reza. *No God but God: The Origins, Evolution, and Future of Islam.* New York: Random House, 2005.

Bennison, Amira. *The Great Caliphs: The Golden Age of the ʿAbbasid Empire.* London: I. B. Tauris, 2009.

Cooperson, Michael, and Shawkat M. Toorawa, eds. *Arabic Literary Culture, 600-925.* Detroit: ThomsonGale, 2004.

Denny, Frederick M. *Introduction to Islam.* 4th ed. Upper Saddle River, N.J.: Pearson Prentice-Hall, 2010.

Elias, Jamal J. *Islam.* Upper Saddle River, N.J.: Prentice-Hall, 2006.

Ernst, Carl W. *The Shambhala Guide to Sufism.* Boston: Shambhala, 1997.

Gregorian, Vartan. *Islam: A Mosaic Not a Monolith.* Washington, D.C.: Brookings Institution Press, 2003.

Hodgson, Marshall G. S. *The Venture of Islam.* 3 vols. Chicago: University of Chicago Press, 1974.

Ibn al-Nadîm. *The Fihrist of al-Nadīm.* Translated by Bayard Dodge. 2 vols. New York: Columbia University Press, 1970.

Kennedy, Hugh. *When Baghdad Ruled the Muslim World.* Cambridge, Mass.: Da Capo Press, 2005.

Lapidus, Ira M. *A History of Islamic Societies.* 2nd ed. Cambridge: Cambridge University Press, 2002.

Lawrence, Bruce B. *New Faiths, Old Fears: Muslims and Other Asian Immigrants in American Religious Life.* New York: Columbia University Press, 2002.

Murata, Sachiko, and William C. Chittick. *The Vision of Islam.* St. Paul: Paragon House, 1994.

Rahman, Fazlur. *Islam.* 2nd ed. Chicago: University of Chicago Press, 1979.

Rippin, Andrew. *Muslims: Their Religious Beliefs and Practices*. 3rd ed. London: Routledge, 2005.

————, ed. *The Islamic World*. New York: Routledge, 2008.

Ruthven, Malise. *Islam in the World*. 3rd ed. New York: Oxford University Press, 2006.

Sells, Michael, ed. and trans. *Early Islamic Mysticism: Sufi, Qur'an, Miʿraj, and Poetical Writings*. New York: Paulist Press, 1996.

Tottoli, Roberto. *Biblical Prophets in the Qur'an and Muslim Literature*. Richmond, Surrey, U.K.: Curzon, 2001.

Watt, William M., and Pierre Cachia. *The Influence of Islam on Medieval Europe*. Edinburgh: Edinburgh University Press, 1996.

2. Qur'an

Abdel Haleem, Muhammad. *Understanding the Qur'an: Themes and Styles*. London: I. B. Tauris, 2010.

Allen, Roger. *The Arabic Literary Heritage*. Cambridge: Cambridge University Press, 1988.

Boullata, Issa J., ed. *Literary Structures of Religious Meaning in the Qur'an*. Richmond, Surrey, U.K.: Curzon, 2000.

Burton, John. *The Collection of the Qur'an*. Cambridge: Cambridge University Press, 1977.

Graham, William A. *Beyond the Written Word: Oral Aspects of Scripture in the History of Religion*. Cambridge: Cambridge University Press, 1987.

Hawting, G. R., and A. A. Shareef, eds. *Approaches to the Qur'an*. London: Routledge, 1993.

Lawrence, Bruce B. *The Qur'an: A Biography*. New York: Atlantic Monthly Press, 2007.

McAuliffe, J. D., ed. *The Cambridge Companion to the Qur'an*. Cambridge: Cambridge University Press, 2006.

Mattson, Ingrid. *The Story of the Qur'an: Its History and Place in Muslim Life*. Oxford: Blackwell, 2008.

Mir, Mustansir. *Understanding the Islamic Scripture*. New York: Pearson Longman, 2008.

Nelson, Kristina. *The Art of Reciting the Qur'an*. New ed. Cairo: American University in Cairo Press, 2001.

Rahman, Fazlur. *Major Themes of the Qur'an*. 2nd ed. With a new foreword by Ebrahim Moosa. Chicago: University of Chicago Press, 2009.

Rippin, Andrew, ed. *The Blackwell Companion to the Qur'an*. Oxford: Blackwell, 2006.

Robinson, Neal. *Discovering the Qur'an: A Contemporary Approach to a Veiled Text*. 2nd ed. Washington, D.C.: Georgetown University Press, 2003.

Sells, Michael. *Approaching the Qur'an: The Early Revelations.* 2nd ed. Ashland, Oreg.: White Cloud Press, 2007.

Tafsîr al-Jalâlayn. Great Commentaries of the Holy Qur'an Series, vol. 1. Translated by Feras Hamza. Louisville: Fons Vitae, 2009.

Turner, Colin. *The Koran: Critical Concepts in Islamic Studies.* New York: Routledge, 2004.

Wadud, Amina. *Qur'an and Woman: Rereading the Sacred Text from a Woman's Perspective.* New York: Oxford University Press, 1999.

Watt, Wm. Montgomery. *Bell's Introduction to the Qur'an.* Rev. and enlarged ed. Edinburgh: Edinburgh University Press, 1977.

3. Muhammad

Armstrong, Karen. *Muhammad: A Prophet for Our Time.* New York: Atlas Books/ HarperCollins, 2007.

Cleary, Thomas. *The Wisdom of the Prophet: The Sayings of Muhammad.* Boston: Shambhala, 2001.

Ernst, Carl W. *Following Muhammad: Rethinking Islam in the Contemporary World.* Chapel Hill and London: University of North Carolina Press, 2003.

Hamidullah, Muhammad. *The Life and Work of the Prophet of Islam.* Edited and translated by Mahmood Ghazi and Mehmood Ahmed. 8th ed. Islamabad: Islamic Research Institute, 1998.

Ibn Ishâq. *The Life of Muhammad: A Translation of Ibn Ishâq's Sîrat Rasûl Allâh.* Translated by Alfred Guillaume. London: Oxford University Press, 1955.

Ibn Saʿd. *Kitâb al-Tabaqât al-kabîr* (The great book of biographies). Translated by S. Moinul Haq. Karachi: Pakistan Historical Society, 1967, 1972.

Kennedy, Hugh. *The Prophet and the Age of the Caliphates: The Islamic Near East from the Sixth to the Eleventh Century.* London and New York: Longman, 1986.

Khalidi, Tarif. *Images of Muhammad: Narratives of the Prophet in Islam across the Centuries.* New York: Doubleday, 2009.

Kulaynî. *al-Kâfî.* Vol. 1. Translated by Muhammad Hasan Rizvi. Karachi: Khurasan Islamic Research Center, 1978.

Peters, F. E. *Muhammad and the Origins of Islam.* Albany: State University of New York Press, 1994.

Rubin, Uri, ed. *The Life of Muhammad.* Brookfield, Vt.: Ashgate, 1999.

Schimmel, Annemarie. *And Muhammad Is His Messenger: The Veneration of the Prophet in Muslim Piety.* Chapel Hill: University of North Carolina Press, 1985.

al-Tabarî. *The History of al-Tabarî.* Vol. 6: *Muhammad at Mecca* (1988); vol. 7: *The Foundation of the Community: Muhammad at Al-Madina* (1987); vol. 8: *The Victory of Islam: Muhammad at Medina* (1997); vol. 9: *The Last Years of the*

Prophet: The Formation of the State (1988). Translated by W. Montgomery Watt, M. V. McDonald, Michael Fishbein, Ismail Poonawala. Albany: State University of New York Press.

Watt, William Montgomery. *Muhammad at Mecca*. Oxford: Clarendon, 1953.

———. *Muhammad at Medina*. Oxford: Clarendon, 1956.

4. Hadith and Sunna

Brown, Jonathan. *The Canonization of al-Bukhari and Muslim: The Formation and Function of the Sunni Hadith Canon*. Leiden: Brill, 2008.

———. *Hadith: Muhammad's Legacy in the Medieval and Modern World*. Oxford: Oneworld, 2009.

al-Bukhârî. *The Translations of the Meaning of Sahih Al-Bukhari: Arabic-English*. Translated by M. M. Khan. 9 vols. Medina: Dar al-Fikr, 1981.

Burton, John. *An Introduction to the Hadith*. Edinburgh: Edinburgh University Press, 2001.

Dickinson, Eerik. *The Development of Early Sunnite Hadith Criticism*. Leiden: Brill, 2001.

Graham, William A. *Divine Word and Prophetic Word in Early Islam*. The Hague: Mouton, 1977.

Juynboll, G. H. A. *Muslim Tradition: Studies in Chronology, Provenance, and Authorship of Early Hadith*. Cambridge: Cambridge University Press, 1983.

Mâlik ibn Anas. *Al-Muwatta of Imam Malik ibn Anas*. Translated by Aisha A. Bewley. London and New York: Kegan Paul International, 1989.

Melchert, Christopher. *Ahmad ibn Hanbal*. Oxford: Oneworld, 2006.

Motzki, Harald. *The Origins of Islamic Jurisprudence*. Translated by Marion H. Katz. Leiden: Brill, 2002.

———, ed. *Hadith: Origins and Developments*. Brookfield, Vt.: Ashgate, 2004.

Muslim ibn al-Hajjâj. *Sahîh Muslim*. Translated by A. H. Siddiqui. 4 vols. Lahore: Sh. Muhammad Ashraf, 1971-75.

al-Nawawî. *Riyad-us-Saliheen (Gardens of the Righteous)*. Translated by M. Amin and A. Usamah bin Razduq. 2 vols. Riyadh: Dar al-Salâm, 1998.

Schoeler, Gregor. *The Genesis of Literature in Islam: From the Aural to the Read*. Rev. ed. in collaboration with and translated by Shawkat M. Toorawa. Edinburgh: Edinburgh University Press, 2009.

al-Shahrazûrî. *An Introduction to the Science of the Hadith*. Translated by Eerik Dickinson. Reviewed by Muneer Fareed. Reading, U.K.: Garnet, 2005.

Siddiqi, M. Z. *Hadith Literature: Its Origin, Development, and Special Features*. 2nd ed. Cambridge: Islamic Texts Society, 1993.

5. Shariʿa

Abdul Rauf, Feisal. *Islam, a Sacred Law: What Every Muslim Should Know about the Shariʿah.* Brattleboro, Vt.: Qiblah Books, 1999.

Amanat, Abbas, and Frank Griffel, eds. *Shariʿa: Islamic Law in the Contemporary Context.* Stanford: Stanford University Press, 2007.

Anderson, J. N. D. *Law Reform in the Muslim World.* London: Athlone Press, 1976.

Averroës. *The Distinguished Jurist's Primer: A Translation of Bidâyat al-Mujtahid.* Translated by I. A. K. Nyazee. 2 vols. Reading, U.K.: Garnet, 1997.

Bearman, Peri J., et al., eds. *The Law Applied: Contextualizing the Islamic Shariʿa.* London: I. B. Tauris, 2008.

Coulson, Noel J. *A History of Islamic Law.* Edinburgh: Edinburgh University Press, 1964.

Hallaq, Wael B. *A History of Islamic Legal Theories: An Introduction to Sunni Usûl al-fiqh.* Cambridge: Cambridge University Press, 1997.

Ibn al-Naqîb. *Reliance of the Traveller: A Classic Manual of Islamic Sacred Law.* Translated by Nuh Ha Mim Keller. Evanston, Ill., and Beltsville, Md.: Amana Publications, 1999.

Kamali, M. H. *Principles of Islamic Jurisprudence.* 3rd rev. enlarged ed. Cambridge: Islamic Texts Society, 2003.

Lowry, Joseph E. *Early Islamic Legal Theory: The Risâla of Muhammad b. Idrîs al-Shâfiʿî.* Leiden: Brill, 2007.

Masud, Muhammad Khaled, et al., eds. *Islamic Legal Interpretation: Muftis and Their Fatwas.* Cambridge: Harvard University Press, 1996.

Mayer, Ann E. *Islam and Human Rights: Tradition and Politics.* Boulder, Colo.: Lynne Rienner, 1999.

Modarressi Tabataba'i, Hossein. *An Introduction to Shiʿi Law: A Bibliographical Study.* London: Ithaca Press, 1984.

Ramadan, Tariq. *Radical Reform: Islamic Ethics and Liberation.* Oxford: Oxford University Press, 2009.

Schacht, Joseph. *An Introduction to Islamic Law.* Oxford: Clarendon, 1964.

Vikør, Knut. *Between God and the Sultan: A History of Islamic Law.* London: Hurst and Co., 2005.

Weiss, Bernard G. *The Spirit of Islamic Law.* Athens: University of Georgia Press, 1998.

6. Islamic Philosophy

Adamson, Peter, and R. C. Taylor, eds. *The Cambridge Companion to Arabic Philosophy.* Cambridge: Cambridge University Press, 2005.

Arkoun, Mohammed. *The Unthought in Islamic Thought.* New York: St. Martin's Press, 2002.

Chittick, William C. *Ibn 'Arabi: Heir to the Prophets.* Oxford: Oneworld, 2005.

Davidson, Herbert A. *Proofs for Eternity, Creation, and the Existence of God in Medieval Islamic and Jewish Philosophy.* Oxford: Oxford University Press, 1987.

————. *Alfarabi, Avicenna, and Averroes, on Intellect.* Oxford: Oxford University Press, 1992.

Fakhry, Majid. *A History of Islamic Philosophy.* 3rd ed. New York: Columbia University Press, 2004.

Frank, Richard. *Beings and Their Attributes, the Teaching of the Basrian School of the Mu'tazila in the Classical Period.* Albany: State University of New York Press, 1978.

al-Ghazâli. *The Incoherence of the Philosophers.* Translated by Michael E. Marmura. 2nd ed. Provo, Utah: Brigham Young University Press, 2002.

Ibn Rushd. *The Incoherence of the* Incoherence. Translated by S. van den Bergh. 2 vols. in 1. Reprint, Cambridge: Gibb Trust, 2008.

Ibn Sîna. *The Metaphysics of* The Healing. Translated by Michael E. Marmura. Provo, Utah: Brigham Young University Press, 2005.

Iqbal, Muhammad. *The Reconstruction of Religious Thought in Islam.* Lahore: Iqbal Academy/Institute of Islamic Culture, 1999.

McGinnis, Jon, and David C. Reisman, trans. *Classical Arabic Philosophy, an Anthology of Sources.* Indianapolis: Hackett, 2007.

Montgomery, James E., ed. *Arabic Theology, Arabic Philosophy.* Leuven: Peeters, 2006.

Mulla Sadra. *The Elixir of the Gnostics.* Translated by William C. Chittick. Provo, Utah: Brigham Young University Press, 2003.

Nasr, Syed Hossein, and Oliver Leaman. *History of Islamic Philosophy.* London: Routledge, 1996.

Soroush, Abdolkarim. *The Expansion of Prophetic Experience: Essays on Historicity, Contingency, and Plurality in Religion.* Translated by Nilou Mobasser. Leiden: Brill, 2009.

al-Suhrawardî. *The Philosophy of Illumination.* Translated by J. Walbridge and H. Ziai. Provo, Utah: Brigham Young University Press, 1999.

Wolfson, H. A. *The Philosophy of the Kalam.* Cambridge, Mass.: Harvard University Press, 1976.

7. Sufism

Baldick, Julian. *Mystical Islam: An Introduction to Sufism.* New York: New York University Press, 1989.

Chittick, William C. *Sufism: A Short Introduction.* Oxford: Oneworld, 2000.

Green, Nile. *Indian Sufism since the Seventeenth Century.* New York: Routledge, 2006.

Heck, Paul L., ed. *Sufism and Politics: The Power of Spirituality.* Princeton: Markus Wiener, 2007.

Karamustafa, Ahmet T. *Sufism: The Formative Period.* Edinburgh: Edinburgh University Press, 2007.

Knysh, Alexander D. *Islamic Mysticism: A Short History.* Leiden: Brill, 2000.

Lewisohn, Leonard, ed. *The Heritage of Sufism.* 3 vols. Boston: Oneworld, 1999.

Malik, Jamal, and John Hinnells, eds. *Sufism in the West.* New York: Routledge, 2006.

Nasr, Syed Hossein. *The Garden of Truth: The Vision and Practice of Sufism, Islam's Mystical Tradition.* New York: HarperOne, 2007.

Renard, John. *Seven Doors to Islam: Spirituality and the Religious Life of Muslims.* Berkeley: University of California Press, 1996.

Ridgeon, Lloyd, ed. *Sufism: Critical Concepts in Islamic Studies.* 4 vols. New York: Routledge, 2008.

Schimmel, Annemarie. *Mystical Dimensions of Islam.* Chapel Hill: University of North Carolina Press, 1975.

Sedgwick, M. J. *Sufism: The Essentials.* Cairo: American University in Cairo Press, 2000.

Shihadeh, Ayman, ed. *Sufism and Theology.* Edinburgh: Edinburgh University Press, 2007.

Sirriyeh, Elizabeth. *Sufis and Anti-Sufis: The Defense, Rethinking, and Rejection of Sufism in the Modern World.* Richmond, Surrey, U.K.: Curzon, 1999.

8. Shi'ites, Shi'ism

Ayoub, Mahmoud. *Redemptive Suffering in Islam: A Study of the Devotional Aspects of 'Ashûra' in Twelver Shi'ism.* The Hague: Mouton, 1978.

Daftary, Farhad. *The Ismai'lis: Their History and Doctrines.* Cambridge: Cambridge University Press, 2007.

Dakake, M. M. *The Charismatic Community: Shi'ite Identity in Early Islam.* Albany: State University of New York Press, 2007.

Halm, Heinz. *Shiism.* Translated by J. Watson and M. Hill. 2nd ed. Edinburgh: Edinburgh University Press, 2004.

Ibn al-Mutahhar al-Hillî. *Al-Bâbu 'l-Hâdi 'Ashar: A Treatise on the Principles of Shi'ite Theology, with Commentary by Miqdad Fadil al-Hilli.* Translated by W. M. Miller. London: Royal Asiatic Society, 1958.

Ibn Bâbawayhi. *A Shi'ite Creed.* Translated by A. A. A. Fyzee. London: Oxford University Press, 1942.

Jafri, S. H. M. *The Origins and Early Development of Shi'a Islam.* New York: Longman, 1979.

Kohlberg, Etan, ed. *Shiism.* Burlington, Vt.: Ashgate, 2003.

Luft, Paul, and Colin Turner, eds. *Shi'ism.* 4 vols. London: Routledge, 2008.

Madelung, Wilferd. *The Succession to Muhammad: A Study of the Early Caliphate.* Cambridge: Cambridge University Press, 1997.

Momen, Moojan. *An Introduction to Shi'a Islam: The History and Doctrines of Twelver Shi'ism.* New Haven: Yale University Press, 1985.

Monsutti, Alessandro, et al., eds. *The Other Shiites: From the Mediterranean to Central Asia.* New York: Peter Lang, 2007.

Newman, Andrew J. *The Formative Period of Twelver Shiism.* Richmond, Surrey, U.K.: Curzon, 2000.

Sachedina, Abdulaziz A. *Islamic Messianism: The Idea of Mahdi in Twelver Shi'ism.* Albany: State University of New York Press, 1981.

Shaykh al-Mufîd. *Kitâb al-Irshâd: The Book of Guidance into the Lives of the Twelve Imams.* Translated by I. K. A. Howard. Elmhurst, N.Y.: Tahrike Tarsile Qur'an, 1981.

Stewart, Devin J. *Islamic Legal Orthodoxy: Twelver Shiite Responses to the Sunni Legal System.* Salt Lake City: University of Utah Press, 1998.

9. Sunnis, Sunnism

Berkey, Jonathan. *The Formation of Islam: Religion and Society in the Near East, 600-1800.* Cambridge: Cambridge University Press, 2003.

Brown, D. W. *Rethinking Tradition in Modern Islamic Thought.* Cambridge: Cambridge University Press, 1996.

Ephrat, Dana. *A Learned Society in a Period of Transition: The Sunni "Ulama" of Eleventh Century Baghdad.* Albany: State University of New York Press, 2000.

Haykel, Bernard. *Revival and Reform in Islam.* Cambridge: Cambridge University Press, 2003.

Hodgson, Marshall G. S. *The Venture of Islam.* 3 vols. Chicago: University of Chicago Press, 1974.

Ibn 'Alawi al-Haddâd, 'Abdallah. *The Book of Assistance.* Translated by Mostafa Badawi. Lexington, Ky.: Fons Vitae, 2003.

Makdisi, George. *The Rise of Colleges in Islam and the Christian West.* Edinburgh: Edinburgh University Press, 1981.

Melchert, Christopher. *The Formation of the Sunni Schools of Law, 9th-10th Centuries C.E.* Leiden: Brill, 1997.

al-Nawawî. *An-Nawawi's Forty Hadith: An Anthology of the Sayings of the Prophet Muhammad.* Translated by Ezzeddin Ibrahim and Denys Johnson-Davies. Cambridge: Islamic Texts Society, 1997.

Ormsby, Eric. *Ghazali.* Oxford: Oneworld, 2008.

Watt, William Montgomery, trans. *Islamic Creeds: A Selection.* Edinburgh: Edinburgh University Press, 1994.

Winter, Tim, ed. *The Cambridge Companion to Classical Islamic Theology.* Cambridge: Cambridge University Press, 2008.

Zaman, Muhammad Qasim. *Religion and Politics under the Early 'Abbâsids: The Emergence of the Proto-Sunni Elite.* Leiden: Brill, 1997.

———. *Ashraf 'Ali Thanawi: Islam in Modern South Asia.* Oxford: Oneworld, 2008.

10. Mosque

Bloom, Jonathan M. *Minaret: Symbol of Islam.* Oxford: Oxford University Press, 1989.

Creswell, K. A. C. *Early Muslim Architecture.* 2 vols. in 3. New York: Hacker Art Books, 1979.

Frishman, M., and H. U. Khan, eds. *The Mosque: History, Architectural Development, and Regional Diversity.* London and New York: Thames and Hudson, 1994.

Hambly, Gavin R. G., ed. *Women in the Medieval Islamic World: Power, Patronage, and Piety.* New York: St. Martin's Press, 1998.

Hillenbrand, Robert. *Islamic Architecture: Form, Function, and Meaning.* New York: Columbia University Press, 1994.

Holod, Renata, and H.-U. Khan, *The Contemporary Mosque: Architects, Clients, and Designs since the 1950s.* New York: Rizzoli, 1997.

al-Jazîrî. *Islamic Jurisprudence according to the Four Sunni Schools.* Vol. 1, *Acts of Worship.* Translated by N. Roberts. Louisville: Fons Vitae, 2009.

Johns, Jeremy, ed. *Bayt al-Maqdis: Jerusalem and Early Islam.* 2 vols. Oxford: Oxford University Press, 1992-1999.

Macaulay, David. *Mosque.* Boston: Houghton Mifflin, 2003.

Parkin, David, and Stephen Headley. *Prayer across the Indian Ocean: Inside and Outside the Mosque.* Richmond, Surrey, U.K.: Curzon, 2000.

Sezgin, Fuat, ed. *The Great Mosque of the Prophet in Medina (al-Haram al-Madani): Texts and Studies.* Frankfurt: Institute for the Study of Arab-Islamic Science, 2007.

Stanley, Tim. *Palace and Mosque: Islamic Art from the Middle East.* London: V & A Publications, 2004.

Talili, Akil. *The Great Mosque of Damascus: From Roman Temple to Monument of Islam.* Damascus: Architectural Research Centre of Old Damascus, 2009.

Wheatley, Paul. *The Places Where Men Pray Together.* Chicago: University of Chicago Press, 2000.

11. Islamic Government

Baderin, Mashood A., ed. *International Law and Islamic Law.* Burlington, Vt.: Ashgate, 2008.

Black, Anthony. *The History of Islamic Political Thought: From the Prophet to the Present.* Edinburgh: Edinburgh University Press, 2001.

Bosworth, C. E. *The New Islamic Dynasties: A Chronological and Genealogical Manual.* Edinburgh: Edinburgh University Press, 1996.

Crone, Patricia. *God's Rule: Government and Islam.* New York: Columbia University Press, 2004.

al-Fârâbî. *Al-Fârâbî on the Perfect State.* Translated by Richard Walzer. New York: Oxford University Press, 1985.

Hourani, Albert. *Arabic Thought in the Liberal Age, 1789-1939.* Cambridge: Cambridge University Press, 1962.

Ibn Khaldûn. *The Muqaddimah: An Introduction to History.* Translated by Franz Rosenthal. Edited by N. J. Dawood. Princeton: Princeton University Press, 1989.

Khomeini, Ruhollah. *Islam and Revolution.* Translated by Hamid Algar. Berkeley, Calif.: Mizan Press, 1981.

Lecker, Michael. *"Constitution of Medina": Muhammad's First Legal Document.* Princeton: Princeton University, 2004.

al-Mâwardî. *The Ordinances of Government.* Translated by Wafaa H. Wahba. Reading, U.K.: Garnet, 1996.

Mottahedeh, Roy P. *The Mantle of the Prophet: Religion and Politics in Iran.* Oxford: Oxford University Press, 2000.

Robinson, Chase. *'Abd al-Malik.* Oxford: Oneworld, 2005.

Sachedina, Abdulaziz. *The Just Ruler (al-sultân al-fâdil) in Shi'ite Islam: The Comprehensive Authority of the Jurist in Imamite Jurisprudence.* New York: Oxford University Press, 1998.

Watt, Wm. Montgomery. *Muhammad: Prophet and Statesman.* Oxford: Oxford University Press, 1961.

12. Women and Islam

Abu-Lughod, Lila, ed. *Remaking Women: Feminism and Modernity in the Middle East.* Princeton: Princeton University Press, 1998.

Afkhami, Mahnaz, ed. *Faith and Freedom: Women's Human Rights in the Muslim World.* Syracuse: Syracuse University Press, 1995.

Ahmed, Leila. *Women and Gender in Islam.* New Haven: Yale University Press, 1992.

Al-Hibri, Azizah, ed. *Women and Islam.* New York: Pergamon Press, 1982.

Ali, Kecia. *Sexual Ethics and Islam: Feminist Reflections on Qur'an, Hadith, and Jurisprudence.* Oxford: Oneworld, 2006.

Cornell, Rkia. *Early Sufi Women: Dhikr an-niswa al-muta'abbidat as-Sufiyyat by Abu Abd ar-Rahman as-Sulami.* Louisville: Fons Vitae, 1999.

Mahmood, Saba. *The Politics of Piety: The Islamic Revival and the Feminist Subject.* Princeton: Princeton University Press, 2005.

Mernissi, Fatima. *The Veil and the Male Elite: A Feminist Interpretation of Women's Rights in Islam.* Translated by Mary Jo Lakeland. Reading, Mass.: Addison-Wesley, 1991.

―――. *The Forgotten Queens of Islam.* Minneapolis: University of Minnesota Press, 1993.

Murata, Sachiko. *The Tao of Islam: A Sourcebook on Gender Relationships in Islamic Thought.* Albany: State University of New York Press, 1992.

Nurbakhsh, Javad. *Sufi Women.* New York: Khaniqahi Nimatullahi Publications, 1983.

Schimmel, Annemarie. *My Soul Is a Woman: The Feminine in Islam.* Translated by Susan H. Ray. New York: Continuum, 1997.

Smith, Margaret. *Muslim Women Mystics: The Life and Work of Rabia and Other Women Mystics in Islam.* Oxford: Oneworld, 2001.

Sonbol, Amira El-Azhary, ed. *Women, the Family, and Divorce Laws in Islamic History.* Syracuse: Syracuse University Press, 1997.

―――, ed. *Beyond the Exotic: Women's Histories in Islamic Societies.* Syracuse: Syracuse University Press, 2005.

Spellberg, Denise A. *Politics, Gender, and the Islamic Past: The Legacy of 'A'isha bint Abi Bakr.* New York: Columbia University Press, 1994.

Stowasser, Barbara. *Women in the Qur'an, Traditions, and Interpretation.* New York: Oxford University Press, 1994.

13. Islam and Judaism

Adang, Camilla. *Muslim Writers on Judaism and the Hebrew Bible: From Ibn Rabbân to Ibn Hazm.* Leiden: Brill, 1996.

Biale, David, ed. *Cultures of the Jews: A New History.* New York: Schocken Books, 2002.

Brann, Ross. *Power in the Portrayal: Representations of Jews and Muslims in Eleventh- and Twelfth-Century Islamic Spain.* Princeton: Princeton University Press, 2002.

Lazarus-Yafeh, Hava, et al., eds. *The Majlis: Interreligious Encounters in Medieval Islam.* Wiesbaden, 1999.

Lecker, Michael. *Jews and Arabs in Pre- and Early Islamic Arabia.* Aldershot, U.K., and Burlington, Vt.: Ashgate, 1998.

Lewis, Bernard. *The Jews of Islam.* London: Routledge, 2008.

Libson, Gideon. *Jewish and Islamic Law: A Comparative Study of Custom during the Geonic Period.* Cambridge: Cambridge University Press, 2003.

Lobel, Diana. *Between Mysticism and Philosophy: Sufi Language of Religious Expe-*

rience in Judah Ha-Levi's Kuzari. Albany: State University of New York Press, 2000.

Lowin, Shari L. *The Making of a Forefather: Abraham in Islamic and Jewish Exegetical Narratives.* Leiden: Brill, 2007.

Perlmann, Moshe. *Ibn Kammuna's Examination of the Three Faiths.* Berkeley: University of California Press, 1971.

Rubin, Uri. *Between Bible and Qur'an: The Children of Israel and the Islamic Self-Image.* Princeton: Darwin Press, 1999.

Scheindlin, Raymond P. *Wine, Women, and Death: Medieval Hebrew Poems on the Good Life.* Philadelphia: Jewish Publication Society, 1986.

Shaw, Stanford J. *The Jews of the Ottoman Empire and the Turkish Republic.* Basingstoke: Macmillan, 1991.

Stillman, Norman A. *The Jews of Arab Lands: A History and Source-Book.* Philadelphia: Jewish Publication Society, 1979.

Tobi, Yoseph, *Proximity and Distance: Medieval Arabic and Hebrew Poetry.* Translated by Murray Rosovsky. Leiden: Brill, 2004.

Wasserstrom, Steven. *Between Muslim and Jew: The Problem of Symbiosis under Early Islam.* Princeton: Princeton University Press, 1995.

14. Islam and Christianity

Bijlefeld, W. A., ed. *Christian-Muslim Relations = Muslim World.* Vol. 88, nos. 3-4. 1998.

Cragg, Kenneth. *The Call of the Minaret.* 2nd revised and enlarged ed. London: Collins, 1986.

Daniel, Norman. *Islam and the West: The Making of an Image.* Edinburgh: Edinburgh University Press, 1960.

———. *The Arabs and Medieval Europe.* American Council of Learned Societies E-Book, 2008.

Gaudeul, Jean-Marie. *Encounters and Clashes: Islam and Christianity in History.* 2 vols. Rome: Pontificio Istituto di Studi Arabi e d'Islamistica, 2000.

Griffith, Sidney H. *The Church in the Shadow of the Mosque: Christians and Muslims in the World of Islam.* Princeton: Princeton University Press, 2007.

Haddad, Yvonne Y., and W. Z. Haddad, eds. *Christian-Muslim Encounters.* Gainesville: University of Florida Press, 1995.

Hoyland, Robert G. *Seeing Islam as Others Saw It: A Survey and Evaluation of Christian, Jewish, and Zoroastrian Writings on Early Islam.* Princeton: Darwin Press, 1997.

———, ed. *Muslims and Others in Early Islamic Society.* Aldershot, U.K., and Burlington, Vt.: Ashgate, 2004.

Miller, Roland E., ed. *Islam = Word & World.* Vol. 16, no. 2. 1996.

Sahas, D. J. *John of Damascus on Islam: The "Heresy of the Ishmaelites."* Leiden: Brill, 1972.

Samir, S. K., and J. S. Nielsen, eds. *Christian Arabic Apologetics during the Abbasid Period (750-1258)*. Leiden: Brill, 1994.

Southern, R. W. *Western Views of Islam in the Middle Ages*. Cambridge: Harvard University Press, 1978.

Tolan, John V. *Saracens: Islam in the Medieval European Imagination*. New York: Columbia University Press, 2002.

Zebiri, Kate. *Muslims and Christians Face to Face*. Oxford: Oneworld, 1997.

15. Islam in America

Bakhtiar, Laleh. *Sufi Women of America: Angels in the Making*. Chicago: Institute for Traditional Psychoethics and Guidance, 1996.

Barboza, Steven, ed. *American Jihad: Islam after Malcolm X*. New York: Doubleday, 1994.

Berg, Herbert. *Elijah Muhammad and Islam*. New York: New York University Press, 2009.

Haddad, Yvonne Y., ed. *The Muslims of America*. New York: Oxford University Press, 1991.

Haddad, Yvonne Y., and Jane I. Smith, eds. *Muslim Communities in North America*. Albany: State University of New York Press, 1994.

Jackson, Sherman A. *Islam and the Blackamerican*. New York: Oxford University Press, 2005.

Kepel, Gilles. *Allah in the West: Islamic Movements in America and Europe*. Translated by Susan Milner. Stanford: Stanford University Press, 1997.

Lincoln, C. Eric. *The Black Muslims in America*. 3rd ed. Grand Rapids: Eerdmans, 1994.

McCloud, Aminah Beverly. *African American Islam*. New York: Routledge, 1995.

Metcalf, Barbara D., ed. *Making Muslim Space in North America and Europe*. Berkeley: University of California Press, 1996.

Muqtedar Khan, M. A. *American Muslims: Bridging Faith and Freedom*. Beltsville, Md.: Amana Publications, 2002.

Nyang, Sulayman S. *Islam in the United States of America*. Chicago: Kazi Publications, 1999.

Poston, Larry. *Islamic Da'wah in the West: Muslim Missionary Activity and the Dynamics of Conversion to Islam*. New York: Oxford University Press, 1992.

Shahid, Athar. *Reflections of an American Muslim*. Chicago: Kazi Publications, 1994.

Smith, Jane Idleman. *Islam in America*. New York: Columbia University Press, 1999.

Turner, Richard Brent. *Islam in the African-American Experience.* 2nd ed. Bloomington: Indiana University Press, 1997.

Waugh, Earl H., et al., eds. *Muslim Families in North America.* Edmonton: University of Alberta Press, 1991.

Wormser, Richard. *American Islam: Growing Up Muslim in America.* New York: Walker and Co., 1994.

Contributors

ROGER ALLEN (D.Phil., University of Oxford) is Professor of Arabic and Comparative Literature at the University of Pennsylvania, where he is also Sascha Jane Patterson Harvie Professor of Social Thought and Comparative Ethics.

RUBA KANA'AN (D.Phil., University of Oxford) is Noor Chair in Islamic Studies at York University.

AHMET T. KARAMUSTAFA (Ph.D., McGill University) is Professor of History and Religious Studies at Washington University in St. Louis.

BRUCE B. LAWRENCE (Ph.D., Yale University) is Nancy and Jeffrey Marcus Humanities Professor of Religion at Duke University.

The late PAUL LÖFFLER was an independent scholar in Lauenberg, Germany.

JOSEPH E. LOWRY (Ph.D., University of Pennsylvania) is Associate Professor of Arabic and Islamic Studies at the University of Pennsylvania.

SCOTT C. LUCAS (Ph.D., University of Chicago) is Assistant Professor of Near Eastern Studies and of Religious Studies at the University of Arizona.

JON MCGINNIS (Ph.D., University of Pennsylvania) is Associate Professor of Philosophy at the University of Missouri–St. Louis.

TAHERA QUTBUDDIN (Ph.D., Harvard University) is Associate Professor of Arabic Literature at the University of Chicago.

ABDULAZIZ SACHEDINA (Ph.D., University of Toronto) is Frances Myers Ball Professor of Religious Studies at the University of Virginia.

JANE I. SMITH (Ph.D., Harvard University) is Senior Lecturer in Divinity and Associate Dean for Faculty and Academic Affairs at Harvard Divinity School.

MARK N. SWANSON (Ph.D., Pontificio Istituto di Studi Arabi e d'Islamistica) is Harold S. Vogelaar Professor of Christian-Muslim Studies and Interfaith Relations at the Lutheran School of Theology at Chicago.

SHAWKAT M. TOORAWA (Ph.D., University of Pennsylvania) is Associate Professor of Arabic Literature and Islamic Studies at Cornell University.

MARK S. WAGNER (Ph.D., New York University) is Assistant Professor of Arabic at Louisiana State University.

HOMAYRA ZIAD (Ph.D., Yale University) is Assistant Professor of Religion at Trinity College.

ARON ZYSOW (Ph.D., Harvard University) is a Fellow of the Institute for the Transregional Study of the Contemporary Middle East, North Africa and Central Asia at Princeton University.

Index

Page numbers in **bold** refer to the glossary.